Gospel Messages from the Antarctic

George Paterson

Scott's First Antarctic Ship
"Discovery" photo by E. Ogden

GOSPEL MESSAGES FROM THE ANTARCTIC

GEORGE PATERSON

GOLDEN KINGDOM PRESS

LAKE HELEN, FLORIDA

Published by Golden Kingdom Press
Lake Helen, Florida, 32744

goldenkingdompress@yahoo.com

ISBN: 978-0-9883280-5-1 - Paperback
ISBN: 978-0-9883280-6-8 - Ebook

Library of Congress Control Number: 2020919552

Printed in the United States of America

CONTENTS

Introduction

Gospel Messages from the Antarctic, was originally published by *Witness and Testimony* in London, England (circa the late 1940's early 50's). The book is a series of talks author George Paterson presented to young people. The stories are based upon the real adventures of Captain Robert Falcon Scott's scientific expedition to the South Pole in 1911.

The spiritual lessons not only appeal to the young, but will also prove to be a help and incentive to those of riper years. Most, if not all, of the principle doctrines of Scripture find expression in the stories in a language which all may readily understand and remember.

Editor's Note

Sometimes we find ourselves at the right time at the right place, and in that ordinary moment, something extraordinary happens that guides us in a new direction, and points the way to the indwelling Christ.

If this book is in your hands, it is meant for you. A message within its pages will speak to your heart. It did mine, back in 1990. One day Mom picked me up at work for lunch. We sat in her car at a fast-food place, eating our sandwiches, facing the traffic. I saw a book in the road, the pages ruffling in the breeze of cars and trucks speeding over it.

Maybe that's a message for me, I thought, with my new-found spiritual awareness. But I was trying to curb it.

"Look at that book in the road!" Mom laughed. "Maybe it's a sign for you." Her comment surprised me. She didn't usually think like that. Waiting for a break in traffic, I jumped out of the car, picked up the ragged blue book and hurried back. The title, *Gospel Messages from the Antarctic,* based on *The Worst Journey in the World*, made me wince...*the worst journey.* Mine had been pretty rough so far. A picture of Captain Scott's ship "Discovery" was inside the cover. I began reading the book that night. The story of the Emperor Penguin and the ice egg was just the lesson needed most.

The book stayed with me through many moves, although mostly forgotten, until the summer of 2020. Inspiration from the Holy Spirit came to reread the old battered book. I was glad I did. The adventure stories and gospel lessons were so timely in dealing with the challenges our world is facing now that it needed to be republished. A way to make the out-of-print book available opened up. Just like Capt. Scott's ship had been stuck in a field of thick pack-ice until the bergs began to break up, and the ship could flow free again.

The last lesson in the book ends with this powerful message:

"When Capt. Scott went to the Pole, he had four companions with him—he certainly could not have arrived there without their help. We must travel together, in company with others who are pressing on in the same way; and perhaps more than anything else, praying together will help us to the goal.

I believe God answers prayer;
I am sure God answers prayer;
I have proved God answers prayer;
Glory to His Name."

Chapter One

THE UNKNOWN LAND

WHO WILL COME EXPLORING?

"*A good land . . . flowing with milk and honey . . .*" (Ex. 3. 8).

"*Christ Jesus my Lord . . .*" (Phil. 3. 8).

THE following stories are based upon incidents recorded in a thrilling book entitled "The Worst Journey in the World" and written by one of the men who went with Capt. Scott in 1911 to the Antarctic Continent. Many of you will have heard of the heroic expedition which ended with the death of Capt. Scott and some of his companions on their way back from the South Pole.

In order that you may all understand the stories, let me first of all tell you something of the conditions of that part of the world.

Do you enjoy very, very cold wintry days in our country, when the ice is thick upon the ponds and the ground is hard as iron, or when snow lies thickly everywhere, or a bitterly cold wind blows that seems to carry your very ears away? You may enjoy the fun of a few such days, but would you like it to be like that all the year round—only very much worse most of the year—with the hottest summer day seldom if ever as warm as our coldest winter day? And how would you like a country where the night in winter and the day in summer is four months long? I am sure you would not like to live under such conditions.

But it is like that on the Antarctic Continent—a great stretch of land in the south of our earth surrounding what is called the South Pole. Not very much is known of it, for only a few explorers have ever visited it. It is a land of ice and snow and howling winds. Where the sea is not frozen, seals and other creatures are found, and strange birds called penguins (you may have seen some at the zoo) live near the water's edge. But on the land, away from the sea, nothing lives at all, either animal or bird or vegetable; it is a barren waste—a wilderness indeed!

Little by little its secrets are being discovered and with the help of aeroplanes the task is becoming easier. But when Capt. Scott and his party went there, they had no aeroplanes to help them and all their journeys had to be made on foot. But in spite of the tremendous difficulties and dangers, they pressed on, and some even died on the way. How nobly those men suffered in a cause that was dear to their hearts! And if you and I could have said to them in the presence of all the perils and trials, 'Do you not think the sufferings too great?' I think they would have answered in a way which would remind us of Paul of old who spoke thus:

"*. . . I go . . . not knowing the things that shall befall me ... save that bonds and afflictions abide me. ... But none of these things move me, neither count I my life dear unto myself, so that I might finish my course . . . and the ministry which I have received . . .*" (Acts 20. 22-24, A.V.)

They suffered courageously—and yet their task was only an earthly one of exploring a new land on the earth which even when discovered seems to be of only small value to men. Paul's task was far, far nobler—that of exploring, and then bringing to other men the knowledge of a *heavenly* land; and that heavenly land was not a barren waste of ice and snow and bitter winds, but a land "flowing with milk and honey"—"*a good land, a land of brooks of water ... a land of wheat and barley and vines and fig trees and pomegranates. . . a land wherein thou shalt eat bread without scarceness, thou shalt not lack anything in it ...*"(Deut. 8. 7-9).

Do you know what that land is? Perhaps you guess Palestine? You would be right in a sense for Palestine is an *earthly* picture of the land referred to. But the land itself is a *heavenly* one, and is none other than the Lord Jesus Christ Himself. A land to explore indeed! What wonders in it! What surprises meet you at every turn! What riches there are! How vast it is! Nobody has ever yet explored it all; and those who know most of it are still pressing on to discover more.

Listen to Paul at the end of his life—the man who perhaps knew more of that heavenly land than any other that has ever lived.

"*... Christ Jesus my Lord ... for whom I suffered the loss of all things ... that I may gain Christ and be found in him . . . that I may know him, and the power of his resurrection, and the fellowship of his sufferings. . . . Forgetting the things which are behind ... I press on toward the goal ...* " 3(Phil. 3. 8-14).

Do you observe the two words "suffered" and "sufferings"?

Must we suffer in learning to know Him?

We may know something of Him without much cost, but the richest treasures and the deepest secrets of that land are only to be found by a costly way. Shall we shrink back because of this? If we are tempted to do so, let us remember how fearlessly Capt. Scott and his men suffered to gain earthly knowledge. How much more worthwhile is the heavenly! And there are always these tremendous promises for us to lay hold of as we go on with our heavenly exploring:

"God is faithful, who will not suffer you to be tempted above that ye are able . . ." (I Cor. 10. 13).

and,

"God is able to make all grace abound unto you; that ye, having always all sufficiency in everything, may abound unto every good work…" (II Cor. 9. 8).

Have you started exploring the land yet?

If not, you will not be able to enjoy or understand fully the stories that we shall share together. Before going any further, will you kneel down and tell the Lord that you want to know Him and to explore the wealthy land that is "in Christ," and ask Him to reveal Himself to your heart? I know he will not turn away from you if you thus seek Him, for He has said "*him that cometh to me I will in no wise cast out*" (John 6. 37).

Now have you done that?

Then come along with me to the Antarctic, and, every time you read of the bitter cold and darkness there, cheer yourself with the thought that "in Christ" there is life and light and comfort and blessing without end.

Now none but Christ can satisfy,
None other name for me:
There's love and life and lasting joy,
Lord Jesus, found in Thee.

Chapter Two

DRIFTING ICE

ARE YOU ON SAFE GROUND?

"I believe that Jesus Christ is the Son of God" (Acts 8. 37).

CAPT. SCOTT and his men travelled as far south as they could possibly go by ship and then landed on Ross Island, where they built their hut and from which they began their exploring. Their principal object was to try to reach the South Pole. The only possible way to it lay across what is called the Great Ice Barrier. This is a great plain of solid ice, of immense thickness and hundreds of miles long and wide, that creeps on its way towards the sea like a very slowly moving river. It travels at the rate of a yard or two a day, so that for practical purposes we can say it does not move at all; at any rate, you would not be afraid of being lost by drifting away to sea on it! Where it reaches the open sea great pieces of it break off and float away as icebergs, leaving the end of it looking like a great cliff of ice.

To get on to the Barrier the explorers had to cross the sea around their island and then climb up. The sea was often frozen and they had to go across on foot; but they never knew quite what to expect, for the condition of the ice sometimes changed very quickly. At times it would be so solid as to seem almost as immovable as the Barrier itself, and then in a very short time it would break up without much warning, and a sudden wind springing up would carry it out to sea, and where there had been seemingly solid ice but a short time before there would be open water.

This fact accounted for one of the earliest adventures that befell some of the explorers. Three men, with four ponies, were traveling over the sea ice. The ice seemed firm and safe, and so at a point the men decided to camp for the night. They tethered their ponies, pitched their tents, and went to sleep. In the middle of the night one of the men was awakened by a noise, and looking out he was horrified to find that the ice all around them had broken up, and they and their camp were floating out to sea on a little island of ice. He wakened his companions and for many hours they worked hard to move their ponies and equipment towards the firm ice of the Barrier, jumping from one island of ice to another as they had opportunity. It was a terrible experience and more than once it seemed as if they must drift out to sea and be lost. But by great efforts they succeeded in reaching the Barrier and saved their lives—though three of their four ponies were unfortunately drowned.

I have not space to give you more of the thrilling details, but you will guess that the men learned from this experience not to trust in treacherous sea ice even though it looked all right. The only safe ice was on the Barrier. Whatever difficulties and dangers there might be there—and there were plenty! —at least there was no risk of drifting away. And besides—the Barrier was the high road to everywhere else that they desired to reach, and if they were to make any progress at all they *must* get on to the Barrier and stay there.

Now all this is true also in the exploration on which you and I agreed in our last talk that we would set out together—to explore that wealthy land called "in Christ." We shall find on our journey what we may call safe Barrier ice and dangerous sea ice, and until we get on to the Barrier and stay there, we shall make no progress in our exploring; we may even drift right away and be lost altogether.

The story of John the Baptist will show what I mean. We first read of him in Matt. 3 (please look it up). What a strong, bold servant of God he was, speaking so fearlessly and confidently to the people! We feel, as we read, that he had made some grand discoveries about the Lord, and that he was standing firmly on absolutely solid ground. Nothing could move him! No fear of his drifting helplessly out to sea!

And, yet when we turn to Matt. 11 (please read it), we find him there an altogether different man. He is doubting and uncertain – not sure where he stands—wondering whether things which he had formerly believed were really true after all. He seems to be adrift—as if the ice under him has broken up and is carrying him away into darkness and despair. We feel we want to shout to him: 'Get off that unsafe ice, John! Run for your life! At any cost get up on the Barrier again: you'll be safe there!'

What had made all the difference?

We shall find the answer in two verses, both of which tell us what John was thinking about the Lord Jesus.

1. John 1. 34. *"I have seen that . . . this is the Son of God."*

2. Matt. 11.3. "*Art thou he that cometh, or look we for another?*"

How confident the first statement is, and how full of doubt the second!

Do you see what has happened to bring John on to such dangerous ice?

He has allowed doubt to lodge in his mind as to who Jesus is.

He began magnificently—"This is the Son of God." The Lord Jesus tells us Himself that this is the really solid ground. (Please find it in Matt. 16). He asked His disciples, "*Who say ye that I am?*" and Peter answered, *"Thou art the Christ, the Son of the living God."* Then Jesus said, "... *upon this rock I will build my church...*" Do you notice what the Lord said—"*this rock?*" Peter was well up on the solid Barrier when he gave that answer! The confession, given right out from his heart, that Jesus was the Son of God was the sure ground and the starting point for everything else. And that is where I want you to begin your exploring.

Ask God to show you in your heart, as He showed to Peter, what it means that Jesus is the Son of God. Say it to yourself again and again. Believe it with all your heart. Believe it even when (as with John the Baptist) it does not seem as if it can be true. Believe it when people around you are denying it and saying that He was only an ordinary man like the rest of us. Never allow a doubt concerning it to lodge in your heart or mind, for the very moment you entertain the doubt you will be on unsafe ice and begin to drift.

Could this be said of just an ordinary man—"*Christ, in whom are hid all the treasures of wisdom and knowledge*"? or this—"*in him dwelleth all the fulness of the Godhead bodily*" (Col. 2. 3, 9)?

Yet these things are said of Jesus—whom we love to call the Lord Jesus Christ. Truly He was not simply a man like other men. He was the very Son of God; and the boy or girl who marvels most at Him, who believes the biggest things about Him, and to whom He is most wonderful, will be the one who goes on into the richest discoveries concerning Him. That is the way to the 'South Pole" for us! The one who has the biggest and most wonderful Lord Jesus will get there first! Shall we not, like Thomas, call Him "*My Lord and my God*" (John 20.28), and cry with Paul "*that I may know him*"—and press toward the goal with all our heart?

Wonderful, wonderful, Jesus is to me.
Counsellor, Prince of Peace, Mighty God is He.
Saving me, keeping me, from my sin and shame,
Wonderful is my Redeemer, praise His Name!

Chapter Three

TRANSPORT DIFFICULTIES

WHAT KIND OF UNDERSTANDING HAVE YOU GOT?

"Be ye not as the horse, or as the mule,

which have no understanding" (Psa. 32. 9).

"The Son of God is come, and hath

given us an understanding" (I. John 5. 20).

OUR explorers went to the Antarctic before aeroplanes were in common use, and every journey made over the ice and snow had to be on foot. Many hundreds of miles were covered during the expedition, often with much danger and suffering, and always with very hard labour and slow progress. In order to help with this part of the work a number of ponies and dogs were used—animals born in cold lands and therefore able to face the severe cold of the Antarctic. Each pony pulled one sledge, but the dogs worked several to a team, being harnessed generally in pairs one behind another and each team pulling a sledge. On the whole, the animals worked well, but they caused many difficulties which could have been avoided if only they had been wiser. But, of course, they were only animals and could not be expected to act as men.

If the spirit of a man could have been put into them, they might have behaved differently—they would have had a new "understanding"—but that could not be done. A horse must always be a horse, a dog can be nothing but a dog. In this there is a very important difference between them and ourselves. A human being need not always be *only* a human being; he or she can become a child of God, with an altogether new nature. So as we go on to see what those animals did, remember that it need not be with us as it was with them. "Be ye not as the horse."

You would scarcely believe how foolishly they acted at times. For example, it was a common habit of the ponies to eat the ropes and straps with which they were tied up, so that often the explorers would have to chase after a pony who had eaten himself free and wandered away. Then again, at the end of the day's journey one of the most necessary tasks of the tired driver in charge of a pony was to build a wall of snow blocks, to shelter the pony from the wind. As often as not, when the man was tucked up comfortably inside his tent, he would hear noises from outside and would go out to find that the pony had kicked down his wall—for no reason at all—and the man would have to build it up again before he could return to his warm sleeping bag. And when he had returned the same thing might happen again! What a stupid pony! "No understanding" indeed!

One pony, named 'Christopher,' gave endless trouble. There was always tremendous difficulty in harnessing him; and then he always refused to start. All the other ponies would set off with their sledges, but Christopher would not move. Then at last he would start off at a run, and on he would go as long as he thought fit, and nothing would make him stop. The poor driver had no option but to keep up with him as well as he could. When at length Christopher did stop, nothing would make him start again until he chose—and then he would repeat the performance. It was of no use giving him orders—he had his own ideas, and these he followed. Again, we say "no understanding"!

The dogs also had their troublesome ways. One of the least was that they were always fighting one another. Then, sometimes, when harnessed to the sledge after a night's rest, they would be very eager to be on the move, and the moment the order to start was given they would race off—but in the wrong direction. Away they would go, taking no notice of the frantic shouts of the driver, and much valuable time and strength would be wasted before at last they were persuaded to settle down steadily in the right direction. And if ever they saw a penguin anywhere near as they were travelling, they would at once turn off in its direction in the hope of catching it—and again time and strength were lost by the whole party. Well, may we say again, "No understanding"!

Now if you could have talked to those ponies and dogs and asked them why they were there, they would no doubt have replied, 'We have come to help the explorers to reach the South Pole.' They might have meant it quite sincerely, but think how they were doing it! At one time they were helping splendidly, and then by some stupid act giving needless trouble that greatly hindered progress. If only they had had a man's nature and understanding instead of an animal's, how much better they could have served!

Now I want you to think of Another who had a team—of men, not dogs—to be with Him in His work. The Lord Jesus when here on earth chose twelve disciples, who went everywhere with Him and to whom He sought to teach His ways. Most of them loved Him and no doubt tried to understand His mind and to do His will. But what mistakes they made!

Please read Luke 9, and you will find there one such failure. Two of the disciples who loved Him most wanted to do a thing in anger which they thought would please Him, but He rebuked them saying, *"Ye know not what manner of spirit ye are of."* Their loyalty to Him was good, but the spirit in them was so different from His Spirit and they therefore could not feel as He felt—their "understanding" was more like that of the ponies and dogs of our story. We can almost hear the pain in His tones because of their foolishness when on another occasion He said to them: *"Do ye not yet perceive, neither understand? Have ye your heart hardened? . . . Do ye not yet understand?"* (Mark 8. 17, 21).

I am sure that often His heart was pained by their folly; and yet how tenderly and patiently He dealt with them! How could they, being sinful men, understand and appreciate the Spirit of God in their Master? They thought and felt as sinful men: He thought and felt as the holy Son of God; and they were in a different world from Him, just as the animals of our story were in a different world from the explorers.

But happily, that was not the end of the matter. After their Master had died and risen again and ascended into heaven, He sent His Spirit to them at Pentecost—you can read of it in Acts 2—and the

Spirit of Jesus entered into them and they became entirely new men, so that everybody around was amazed at the change. Now they could think and feel as their Master Himself—they might have said, in the words of our text, *"The Son of God is come, and hath given us an understanding."*

They had received a new nature; the Holy Spirit had brought their Master *into* them—no longer merely *with* them—and had taken full possession of their hearts and lives; and they were glad to let Him do whatsoever He desired in and with them. And it is remarkable how they began at once to understand the things of Christ which had previously been so difficult for them.

Thank God, you and I can have a similar experience—indeed we *must* do so if we are going to make any discoveries in the land called "In Christ" which we have set out to explore. If we follow our own ideas or rely upon our own understanding, we shall make no advance whatever. *We must receive a new nature*—that is what Jesus meant when He said, *"Except a man be born again (or born from above) he cannot see the kingdom of God"* (John 3. 3) And *we must allow that new nature to govern us in all things,* even when it leads us in ways which our own nature would not choose to follow. That is what the Lord meant when He said: "*If any man would come after me let him deny himself . . . and follow me*" (Matt. 15. 24).

Have you been "born from above" yet? If not, the Lord Jesus is ready at this moment to come into your heart if you will open it to Him— "*to as many as received him to them gave he the right to become children of God*" (John 1. 12). Then if you are willing to follow Him humbly in all things, His spirit will guide you step by step into all the truth, taking of the things of Christ and showing them to you. The one who yields to the Holy Spirit most will be the first to reach the 'South Pole' of our exploring. Until our next talk together, please often pray the following prayer:

> More about Jesus let me learn,
> More of His holy will discern;
> Spirit of Christ my teacher be,
> Showing the things of Christ to me.

Chapter Four

BLIZZARDS

HAVE YOU SEEN THE WAY HOME?

"We behold . . . Jesus, . . . crowned . . ."

(Heb. 2. 9).

"Run . . . the race . . . looking unto Jesus . . ."

(Heb. 12. 1, 2).

"I was not disobedient unto the heavenly vision"

(Acts 26. 19).

ONE of the greatest dangers of Antarctic exploring is the blizzard. Often, with little warning, the snow begins to fall so thick and fast that a man cannot see his hand held out at arm's length. This is how our book describes a blizzard:

'Outside the tent there is raging chaos. It is blowing a full gale: the air is full of falling snow, and the wind drives this along and adds to it the loose snow which is lying on the surface of the ice. Fight your way a few steps away from the tent, and the tent will be lost to sight. Lose your sense of direction and there is nothing to guide you back . . ..'

One of our explorers nearly lost his life in such a blizzard. It was in the dark night and bitter cold of winter. He went out of the hut where the party lived, in order to attend to one of the scientific instruments that was fixed in the ice of the frozen sea not far away. A blizzard was blowing, but he thought he could safely make so short a journey, and so he set out. After walking about two hundred yards, however, he decided that conditions were so bad he had better turn back, and he did so, walking as he thought exactly in the direction from which he had come. After a while, to his surprise, he found himself not back at the hut but close to an object on the ice which he recognized, and which he knew was some distance from the shore and not in his proper direction at all. He turned in what he thought must be the right direction, but he could see nothing, for the snow was like a thick blanket all round him, and it was quite dark. He walked on and on—and realized that he was completely lost.

'Hour after hour he staggered about, stumbling, tumbling, tripping, buffeted by the wind, sprawling through miles of punishing snow. He found an island, spent ages coasting along it, then lost it . . .; he found another island (perhaps it was the same one again, he could not tell) and the same horrible, almost senseless, search went on ...'

All this time he was being more and more numbed by the intense cold; his hand was frost bitten, his feet nearly so. There was little chance of saving his life if the blizzard continued; but hope revived when the snow eased for a brief period and he saw the moon. He remembered having seen it shining the previous night, and from its position in the sky he could make a rough guess at the direction in which the hut should be. So he set off; but the blizzard came down again and blotted out the moon once more. He stumbled on and found another island (was it the same one again?) and waited. Again, came a lull, and the moon; and on he went. At last he saw a light burning. He went straight towards it—and found himself home at last. The light had been lighted by his friends at the hut who had been anxiously awaiting his return. When his troubles began, he was only two hundred yards from the hut, but it had taken him over six hours to reach home and he found later that one of the islands he had been traveling round was as much as four miles away.

It was seeing and following the light that saved him. He had thought he knew the way, he had tried to work out his own course, he had relied upon his memory, and used his wits to the best of his ability; but these were not able to bring him to his goal. A light altogether outside of himself and different from his own thoughts and ideas had to shine for him, and when he followed *that* light all was well.

As a young man the apostle Paul (then named Saul) had an experience very like this. He set out on life's journey, and the one place he wanted to reach—the one thing he wanted to do—was to serve God as he ought. He thought he knew the way and he followed it quite confidently to begin with; but we have reason to think that after a while, like our explorer, he began to wonder if he was on the right track after all. But he pressed on, always hoping that he would reach the desired end. He did some extraordinary things in his efforts to serve God—he even persecuted and killed the followers of the Lord Jesus! He was quite sincere—he says, "*I verily thought that I ought . . .*" (Acts 26.9).

It shows us how a man can be in the dark, like the explorer in the blizzard, thinking he is going the right way and not knowing how far astray he is. But Saul did eventually reach 'home' safely. What showed him the way there? Did someone talk to him and convince him he was wrong? Did he sit down and read in the Scriptures that he ought not to do certain things? Not at all—the remarkable thing is that he knew the Scriptures thoroughly and read them constantly, and thought he was acting in accordance with their teaching. Yes, he verily thought that he ought . . .! But his thoughts, even about God's Word, were wrong and led him astray. When he began to realize this, there must have been with him, as with our explorer, a deep cry in his heart for a light to shine and show him the right way. And then one day, quite suddenly, he saw a light—and he followed it and found he was 'home.' His wanderings were over. He had suddenly come into the light of *God's* thoughts instead of his own, and everything was changed. You can read the story of it in the book of Acts, chapters 9, 22 and 26.

What did he see?

It was more than just a light—it was a Person; none other than the Lord Jesus Christ Himself in heaven. Paul afterwards called what he saw, "the heavenly vision." What he saw with his physical eyes soon faded away, but with the eyes of his heart he continued to look upon it for the rest of his life—he was always beholding Jesus, crowned. As he thought and prayed about it, its meaning grew more and more wonderful to him, and as he followed what he saw it seemed as if the light grew *in* him as well as before him. So in writing once about his experiences he said, "it pleased God. . . to reveal his Son *in* me" (Gal. 1. 15, 16). He saw more and more how foolish were his own thoughts, and he gladly let them go and followed the new light wherever it led and whatever it cost.

That is what he meant by saying, *"I was not disobedient unto the heavenly vision."*

Now I cannot even begin here to tell you the meaning of what Paul saw. But it is of the greatest importance that we should follow his example. We shall certainly not see the Lord Jesus with our physical eyes as Paul did, but with the eyes of our heart we may and must see Him. Here are some things we can do about it:

(1) Humble our hearts before God and tell Him that we need His light to guide us 'home.'

(2) Resolve that so far as we know how to do it, we will "run . . . the race, . . . looking unto Jesus."

(3) Ask God to open the eyes of our heart so that we may really see "the heavenly vision" for ourselves.

(4) Ask Him to show us more and more what that vision means, and to give us grace to be obedient to it, whatever it may cost.

Will you do this? He or she who most clearly sees and follows the heavenly vision will reach the 'South Pole' first.

Turn your eyes upon Jesus,
Look full in His wonderful face;
And the things of earth will grow strangely dim
In the light of His glory and grace.

Chapter Five

FOOD SUPPLIES

ARE YOUR RATIONS RUNNING SHORT?

Jesus said: "I am the living bread. . ." (John 6. 51).

"Christ in you, the hope . . ." (Col. 1. 27).

FOOD was the great problem in the Antarctic. While the explorers moved on or near the sea, there was always the chance of killing a seal or a penguin for food, but inland there was no living thing whatever to be found—not even a blade of grass. They were compelled to take with them every ounce of food needed. This involved some very careful planning. It would have been easy if they had merely to calculate how much would be needed by so many men travelling for a certain number of days, if each man were to have so much food each day; but it was much more complicated than that.

Their great object was to reach the South Pole, a total distance from their base of about 1,700 miles. They could not possibly take with them all the food needed for such an immense distance, and a most careful plan was made for meeting the need. First of all, a party of men went out a considerable distance to make depots, or dumps, of food. This in itself was a long and difficult and dangerous journey. Then later, a party of sixteen men with dogs and ponies, set out, all pulling food on their sledges. At certain stages some food–very carefully calculated—was dumped to provide for the return journey. Later, after careful calculation of quantities, the ponies were killed one by one because they were no longer needed and their flesh was required for feeding the dogs. At a certain point—again very carefully planned, and having regard to the amount of food available—some of the men and the dogs turned back for home. Further on, others turned back, leaving only five men to travel the last 150 miles to the Pole.

What a business it must have been calculating in advance how much of each kind of food must be taken! If you were set to do a sum like that at school, I think you would give it up as hopeless. And remember—any mistake made might mean the death of the men concerned. Some of our explorers did almost die of starvation on the way back, and they must often have been in great anxiety wondering if their stocks would last out. At times they were held up for days by blizzards, and had to eat the precious stores that had been set aside for the journey, without any hope of replacing them. The great tragedy of the whole expedition was this—that the five men who went on did reach the Pole, but on the way back two died from exhaustion, and later the other three died of starvation at a point where they were actually only eleven miles from a dump where they could have had all that they needed.

Oh, what a heartbreak this matter of food must have been to them! Never-ending calculations of what was needed, and never-ending anxiety whether there would be enough to meet the need! Our explorers were brave men and did not worry needlessly; but how often they must have asked themselves questions: 'Shall we have enough? Ought we to reduce our rations? Suppose we are delayed by a blizzard? Dare we go on further or should we turn back in case?'

What a world of uncertainty to live in! If only they could have started out with supplies that did not grow less and less! If only they could have eaten food which satisfied all their need and yet was there for use at the next meal! That would have solved their transport difficulties. But it could not be. They ate food that perished—not "living bread."

Now you and I have agreed to go exploring in the land called "In Christ," and there we too have need of food—but spiritual, not material, food. Are we going to be worried and made anxious all the time by questions: 'How. . .? What. . .? Where. . .? Supposing...? Is it safe to go on? Shall we be able to get through?'

Oh, what a miserable world to live in! Many people, even Christians, do live in it and they are not helpful or happy. They are not restful; they have no confidence. Life for them is a great strain. Compare them with what the Lord Jesus said: *"Be not anxious...what ye shall eat, or what ye shall drink, nor ...what ye shall put on"* (Matt. 6. 25).

How restful He Himself was! He was never fretted or anxious. He knew the secret of *always having enough for every need.* He described it in this strange way: *"the living Father sent me and I live because of the Father"* (John 6. 57). He meant this:

'My Father, Who is the Living One, is the source of my life: He satisfies every need of mine: I do not have to depend on things outside of myself—the Father is *in* me and I feed on Him, I live by Him.'

How restful to know that all you need is inside you—that you have it with you wherever you go, and that no matter how much you draw upon it there is always enough for all future needs, however great and unexpected they may be!

You do not have to ask, 'How shall I get through? What shall I do if. . .?'

All that you need is inside! Is such a life of rest possible for us? Yes, indeed it is, or the Lord Jesus would not have said:

"Be not anxious ..."

He Himself is the way to it; and the secret lies in *having Him inside;* and this is possible only to people who have been born from above. When we are born from above, the Lord Jesus, by His Spirit, comes to dwell within us, and He is there all the time for us to feed on, and to be the answer to every need of ours.

So He said: *"As the living Father sent me, and I live because of the Father; so he that eateth me, he also shall live because of me"* (John 6. 57). *"I am the bread which came down out of heaven"* (6. 51). *"I am the bread of life; he that cometh to me shall not hunger, and he that believeth on me shall never thirst"* (6. 35). The bread of life—*living* bread! No need for supplies of that to run short; however much we use there is plenty more!

As to water, our explorers did not need to carry that with them—there was plenty of snow everywhere which they could melt and drink; but the spiritual water which you and I need in our exploring does not even have to be collected from outside.

Here it is: *"Whosoever drinketh of the water that I shall give him shall never thirst; but the water that I shall give him shall become in him a well of water springing up unto eternal life*" (John 4. 14). A well inside us that can never run dry!

If we know the secret of feeding on Christ and drinking of the water that He gives, all our anxious questions disappear and we can say with Paul, "*I can do all things . . . I have all things . . .*" (Phil. 4. 13, 18). We need not hesitate to step out, to move into the unknown, to attempt tasks too hard for us, if the Lord bids us to go forward. We need not wonder whether our supplies will come to an end and we shall be stranded. We may dare *anything* at His bidding. We may trust Him in *any* circumstances. He is always sufficient.

Our *own* resources will certainly come to an end very quickly, but the moment we turn to the Lord and in faith rely upon Him as within us, we shall find we have an inexhaustible supply—we live because of Him.

You will understand of course that we cannot count on His help in doing things that He does not want us to do, but apart from this every need will be met, and even when the next step forward looks difficult, we need not worry—Christ in us will be the answer.

But can we trust Him like that? Will *you* depend on Him like that, for every need of every day?

It will not happen apart from your faith. "*All things are possible to him that believeth*" (Mark 9. 23). That is what is meant by "eating" Christ and living because of Him.

Surely the boy or girl who knows most really the secret of "*Christ in you*" (Col. 1. 27) will be the one who will reach the 'South Pole' first.

I'm feeding on the living bread,
I'm drinking at the fountain head,
And whoso drinketh, Jesus said,
Shall never, never thirst again.

Chapter Six

THE PONIES

ARE YOU LOSING BY KEEPING OR KEEPING BY LOSING?

"He that loveth his life loseth it;
and he that hateth his
Life in this world shall
keep it unto life eternal"
(John 12. 25).

IN our last talk together, we spoke of the great difficulty of food supplies in the Antarctic, and said that the ponies which were used in pulling the sledges on the journey to the South Pole were later killed in order to provide food for the dogs. Perhaps you felt very sorry about that and wished the ponies could have come back alive. But had they done so they would not have served the expedition so well.

The real truth is that their death was no accident; for when Capt. Scott was planning what was needed in the way of stores, transport, etc., before ever he set out from his country at all, he decided to take the ponies and to kill them when they had done their work. He knew how hard it would be to arrange food supplies on the journeys over the ice and snow. He wanted the ponies' help in pulling the sledges loaded with food, and he knew that at a certain point the best help they could give to the whole expedition would be to give up their lives so that their flesh could be used for feeding others—dogs and men. And so, he calculated carefully how far he required to take the ponies and when they should die. So although they did not know it, the ponies went to the Antarctic on purpose to labour, to suffer and then to die.

It was a sad business for all concerned. The journey over the ice was very difficult, and the ponies suffered greatly. They grew weaker and weaker, but they struggled on bravely. Gradually their strength—or the food available for them—came to an end, and there was nothing for it but to kill the ponies. Jehu was the first to be shot; then Chinaman; then Christopher, the pony who had been a continual trouble from the beginning. Even after he had been shot, instead of dying on the spot he charged away, bit one of the men, and had to be recaptured and led back to the place of execution. He was not going to die if he could help it. Then followed Victor; then Michael, who had the awkward habit of eating anything he could get hold of, including the rope that tethered him and the rug that covered him.

The remaining ponies, after terrible hardships, reached the appointed end of their journey, and there, at a place, which the men called 'Shambles Camp,' they were killed—Jimmy Pigg, Snatcher, Nobby, Bones, and Snippets. They had been a gallant, though troublesome, team and had finished their task. They had worked hard and suffered much. If they could have chosen for themselves, they would not have died, but their lives were taken unwillingly from them and their flesh became a very valuable addition to the store of food for the men and dogs who had still to complete the journey.

Christopher was always a nuisance—he never would do what was required of him. But if by some means he could have been made to know that at the end of his labor and suffering he was to give up his life for the sake of others, I think he would have been more troublesome still and would have refused to go forward at all. So would the other ponies; and so, I fear, would you and I. We all want to keep our lives, not to lose them. And that brings me to the point of this story.

The Lord Jesus Christ toiled as hard as any man in the world; He suffered more than any other; but one of the things in which He was so different from every other man was this, that *He came into the world on purpose to die for others.* It was always before Him. He said that He had come "*not to be ministered unto, but to minister, and to give his life a ransom for many*" (Mark 10. 45).

You know how He did die—by being crucified by wicked men. It looked as if they took away His life, just as the explorers took away the ponies' lives. But this was not so.

Men could have had no power over Him if He had not given Himself into their hands.

He said: "*I am the good shepherd. . . I lay down my life for the sheep. . . .No one taketh it away from me, but I lay it down of myself*" (John 10. 14, 15, 18).

He did not die as the ponies did—because He could not help it; but He deliberately decided and chose to die. This is a great mystery—the mystery of infinite love; for He came into the world to save sinners, and He could save them only by dying for them. If He had loved His own life and had desired to keep it, He would have turned back and never completed the work His Father had given Him to do. But He steadfastly set His face to go to Jerusalem, knowing that He was to give up His life there – that 'Shambles Camp' for Him was to be the place of the Cross. And there, having finished His work, He willingly laid down His life.

"Greater love hath no man than this, that a man lay down his life for his friends" (John 15. 13). The Lord Jesus did more than that—*"while we were enemies. . . while we were yet sinners, Christ died for us"* (Rom. 5. 10, 8).

Now 'laying down the life' does not necessarily mean dying in the ordinary sense of that word. It may include that for some people, but probably not for most of us. But it does mean something that affects us all very closely. It means letting go our own rights and wishes and desires – seeking the good of others even at cost to ourselves –going God's way instead of our own—saying No to self and Yes to God in everything—taking 'I' to the Cross and reckoning it as dead.

Paul called this 'dying daily'; it was not the death of the body so much as the death of self. The Lord Jesus did this every moment of His life here, and the final act of His self-denial was to give His very body to be crucified for our sakes. This 'dying daily' is what He meant when He spoke of a man '*hating his life'* (John 12. 25); or *'losing his life'* (Matt. 10. 39); or '*denying himself*' (Luke 9. 23).

You will probably say at once 'I could not do that, I love my life too much.' Exactly—that is our trouble; and it is serious, because our text tells us that "he that loveth his life loseth it." But the Lord Jesus has commanded us to do as He did and to love as He loved. How can we hope to follow His example if it means 'dying daily'?

Well, He Himself is the answer to that problem, as to every other. For He not only said, *"I lay down my life,"* but He also said, *"and I have power to take it again"* (John 10. 18). Having given up His life, He rose again from the dead; and the life with which He rose He is able to share with others. It is this very life which He now gives to every one who is born from above. It is His own love-life. By this life we can do as He has done. We can love others; we can "deny" or "hate" ourselves; we can love God's will; we can say with Paul, *"Neither count I my life dear unto myself, so that I might finish my course with joy"* (Acts 20. 24). Please notice those two words—"with joy." For we must not think of this way as one of only suffering and loss and sorrow. It has wonderful compensations even now.

Why, only a few hours before He was crucified the Lord Jesus spoke of His own peace and joy (John 14. 27; 15. 11), and these He gives to those who follow Him in the way of the Cross. These are the first rewards of following Him. And they are by no means all.

Don't forget that Nobby, Jimmy Pigg and the rest—even cantankerous old Christopher—by dying became food for others, and they teach us that even a life unwillingly laid down can be a blessing of a kind to others.

How much more may we be a blessing if, by the enablement of the love-life of our Lord Jesus working within us, we gladly lay down our lives for others!

Moreover, the blessing that the ponies left by their death was very soon ended—all that can be said is that their flesh helped to keep the dogs and men alive until in their turn they died; and five of the men died only three months later—but the blessing that we receive and the blessing that we give to others by following the Lord Jesus in the laying down of our lives does not end with life in this world, but goes on for ever—for He said, "*He that hateth his life in his world shall keep it unto life eternal*" (John 12. 25).

The boy or girl who follows the Lord Jesus most closely in this way of the life laid down will certainly be the first to reach the 'South Pole' of the land "In Christ" which we are exploring. Will you pray that you may have grace to follow Him thus? Here is a prayer which He will surely answer if you pray it from your heart:

O Saviour, loving Redeemer,
Saviour, precious to me,
Grant me, I pray Thee, more of Thy Spirit,
So that Thy love flows freely through me.

Chapter Seven

CREVASSES—HOW TO KEEP OUT

ARE YOU AFRAID OF FALLING IN?

"Why are ye fearful, O ye of little faith?"
(Matt. 8. 26).

"Fear not, only believe"
(Mark 5. 36).

CREVASSES were a continual trouble to our explorers. A crevasse is a crack in the surface of the ice. Sometimes it may be only a few inches wide and deep, so that it really is not a serious danger at all. But sometimes it may be yards wide, and so deep that you cannot see to the bottom of it. If a man fell into such a crack, he would almost certainly never be brought up again alive.

But the worst crevasses are not the ones that can be seen. After all, with a certain amount of trouble you could probably avoid those. But very many cannot be seen. In the Antarctic, where snow very often falls, it is quite a common thing for a layer of frozen snow gradually to settle over the top of a crevasse—even a big one—completely hiding it. If you were to walk over the bridge of snow thus formed it might bear your weight and you would get safely over without knowing that you had crossed a crevasse; but if the bridge gave way, down you would suddenly go. Happy for you if it were not a deep crevasse, so that you could scramble, or be pulled out, again!

Nowadays, explorers in the Antarctic do most of their journeys by aeroplane, so that crevasses do not trouble them very greatly. But in Capt. Scott's day aeroplanes had scarcely been thought of, and every yard that he and his men travelled had to be on foot. Literally thousands of miles were covered over the ice, the explorers taking their provisions with them on sledges which were pulled either by the men themselves or by ponies or dogs. They often covered the same routes, and learned after a time in which areas the crevasses were worst, and they of course avoided those areas as much as possible. But even in what they thought were safe areas they often stumbled into one. They could never assume that there was none, and needed to be always watchful. But some areas, even though known to be badly crevassed, simply had to be crossed again and again as there was no other way forward, and either the explorers must go on and take the risk or turn round and admit defeat and go home.

On one occasion a team of dogs, harnessed one behind the other and drawing a sledge, were running steadily forward without any particular danger apparent, when suddenly they disappeared one by one, just like dogs following one another down a hole after some animal. They had fallen into a crevasse, and if the explorers had not acted very quickly the whole party—dogs, men and sledge—might have been lost.

On another occasion, one man fell into crevasses eight times in 25 minutes! Happily, his companions were able to rescue him each time.

How would you like travelling over such ground? Would you go restfully forward without being afraid, or even anxious—or would you be too nervous to venture at all?

For an explorer to arrive home and have to say, 'I did not make any discoveries because I was afraid to go forward in case I fell into a crevasse,' would have been a poor confession to make, and most people would call him a coward. Not one of Capt. Scott's men was like that; but I am not so sure about us Christians. Are we not very often afraid to go on?

Afraid of what?

Why, that if we do what we know God wants us to do we may find ourselves in trouble. And Satan is only too ready to make us afraid. He whispers all kinds of doubt into our hearts, trying by any means to convince us that it is not safe to trust God. Shame on us that we listen so readily to his voice!

Do you remember how the children of Israel listened to that voice when their spies came back and reported what they had seen in the land of Canaan?

The spies said that it was truly a good land but that they had seen giants there; and then they said, *"We are not able to go up against the people; for they are stronger than we"* (Num. 13. 31). Caleb and Joshua—men who were ready to trust God—said, *"Let us go up at once and possess . . . for we are well able to overcome. . . .If the Lord delight in us, then he will bring us into this land, and give it unto us"* (13. 30; 14.8). But the fainthearts won, and made the rest of the people afraid to go forward, with the result that they all died in the wilderness. What terrible consequences may follow if we are afraid to trust God!

You will remember another scene—a great Philistine giant defying all the armed men of Israel, who, when they saw him, "*fled from him and were sore afraid*" (I. Sam. 17. 24). And there was a young shepherd lad standing by, named David, who said to the king, "*Let no man's heart fail because of him; thy servant will go and fight with this Philistine. . . . The Lord . . .will deliver me . . .*" (17. 32, 37). And, trusting in the Lord, David went forward, slew the giant and delivered Israel.

What tremendous blessing may come to many if only one will dare to trust God! It was this same David who later wrote: "*What time I am afraid, I will put my trust in thee. . . . In God have I put my trust, I will not be afraid*" (Psa. 56. 3, 11).

You will remember also the children of Israel at the Red Sea, with the Egyptian army pursuing them. God opened a way through the sea, causing the waters to divide, and to be "*a wall unto them on their right side and on their left*" (Ex. 14. 22).

Suppose some poor timid Israelite had said, 'I am not going to venture between those walls of water in case they fall on me before I have got across.' Well, he would have been captured by the Egyptians and would never have known the joy of liberty—just because he was afraid to trust God.

This manner of daring to trust God is so important. Our Christian life is really very much like that of the explorers moving among crevasses. There are plenty of possible dangers and difficulties to be faced. The seen ones can often be avoided by walking carefully. But there are many that we cannot see.

What shall we do about those?

We must be careful not to make the mistake that Peter made, thinking that *he* would never get into trouble. Do you remember his confident words? *"Even, if I must die with thee, yet will I not deny thee"* (Matt. 26. 35).

But very soon afterwards an unseen 'crevasse' opened beneath his feet and he had an awful fall, from which only the Lord Whom he had denied could deliver him. *"Let him that thinketh he standeth take heed lest he fall."*

But if we are not like Peter, we must equally not go to the other extreme and say, 'Because I cannot see all the hidden difficulties, I will not move at all lest I fall into a crevasse.'

Do you know what God wants you to do over some matter?

Then you can quite safely go forward in that direction *if you do so trusting in Him and not in yourself.* He will carry you safely over all the dangerous places, and you need not be afraid. You cannot trust God and be afraid at the same time. Which would you rather do?

Surely it is better to have a trusting heart than a fearing one?

It is sheer misery to live in continual fear of what may happen, at every step in life saying to yourself, as it were, 'I am afraid I am going to fall into a crevasse this time.'

Many men in the Bible show us the blessedness of the man who trusts in the Lord, but none so well as our Lord Jesus Himself. In everything that He did and everywhere that He went, He was trusting entirely in His Father. His trust was perfect, without a trace of doubt or fear. His enemies laid traps for

Him again and again, hoping that He would fall into them. He never ran foolish risks and walked always very carefully; but beyond that, He knew that He could quite safely trust Himself to His Father's care so long as He did only the things that please His Father—and He was thus the most carefree man that ever lived. His heart and mind were in perfect peace because He trusted. And among the precious words that He spoke to His disciples before He left them were these:

"My peace I give unto you. . . Let not your heart be troubled, neither let it be fearful" (John 14. 27).

How can He give His peace to others?

In the same way that He gives all else that He possesses—by giving *Himself* to those who believe in Him and being with them in the way that they take. *"Lo, I am with you alway . . ."* He has said (Matt. 28. 20). Having His Spirit within us, and the Lord Jesus Himself walking with us as our companion and guide, we shall find that the most dangerous path becomes safe, however many 'crevasses' may lie in it, and we may go boldly forward wherever God leads us. Remember that He is the One Who walked on the sea, and enabled Peter to do the same (Matt. 14. 25-31). He can surely take us safely across the snow-bridge of a hidden crevasse!

Are you one of the fainthearts who is afraid to trust God?

You will never make any progress if you are. The boy or girl who trusts God most will reach the 'South Pole' before others. Away, then, with those fears of yours! Turn your eyes upon the calm, strong, confident face of the Lord Jesus, and say to Him from your heart, 'Lord, by thy grace I will trust and not be afraid and I will follow Thee withersoever Thou goest.'

Trusting as the moments fly,
Trusting as the days go by,
Trusting Him whate'er befall,
Trusting Jesus, that is all.

Chapter Eight

CREVASSES—HOW TO GET OUT

WILL YOUR HARNESS BEAR THE STRAIN?

"Jesus said, I give unto them eternal life; and they shall never perish . . ." (John 10. 28).

"Lay hold on eternal life" (I. Tim. 6. 12).

IN our last story we were speaking of crevasses, those cracks in the ice which were a constant danger to the explorers. Although every effort was made to avoid them, on many occasions, men fell in; but the remarkable thing was that in spite of the many falls not one man was killed or seriously hurt. The explanation was that the men did not go without a companion in the areas where there were likely to be crevasses, and almost always they travelled roped to their sledges; that is to say, they wore what they called harness, to which was attached a rope, the other end of the rope being tied to the sledge. This enabled them when necessary to pull the sledge, but it also acted as a safeguard in case they fell.

You can imagine what frequently happened. The men would be travelling over the ice when suddenly one of them would disappear down a crevasse. If it were a deep one, he would fall, and then suddenly stop with a jerk as he reached the full length of the rope by which he was tied to the sledge. It would cause a tremendous strain upon the rope and his harness and, if there were any weak places in either, the sudden jerk would almost certainly result in a break, and then there would be nothing to prevent the man from falling to the bottom of the crevasse, and probably being killed. But if the rope were strong, the man would remain hanging safely but uncomfortably in mid-air. If, in a moment of alarm, he began to struggle to save himself, he would probably do no good at all, but on the other hand he might either break the rope or accidentally slip out of his harness and fall to his death. No, the only thing to do would be to remain quietly there, laying hold of the rope and trusting in it and in the sledge to hold him safe, and waiting patiently until his companions came to the rescue. Fretting and struggling would not help at all. Quietness and confidence would be the wiser and more helpful course.

Here is the description of one incident:

"*Lashly dropped into a crevasse. He fell to the length of his rope and harness. I was glad that, having noticed his rope rather worn, I had given him a new one a few days before. He jerked Crean and me off our feet backwards . . . and pulled the sledge half across the crevasse. I was a little afraid of sledge and all going down, but fortunately it held. We could not see Lashly . . . but we eventually pulled him up.*"

Of course, if the sledge itself had fallen there would have been no hope for anyone, as its weight would have pulled all the men with it to the bottom of the crevasse. Everything depended upon the sledge remaining on the firm ice. Happily, not once in all the expedition did a sledge fall into a dangerous crevasse, nor did a rope or harness break at a critical moment.

Now, other people besides Antarctic explorers may suddenly fall into 'crevasses,' however carefully they may seek to walk. We all know something about such falls in our ordinary daily life. I said in our last story that if we put our trust in the Lord and not in ourselves, He will carry us safely over all the dangerous 'crevasses' we may have to cross.

I ought to say, however, that there are times when, instead of taking us safely across, He allows us to fall in—not because He wants us to be swallowed up, but because He sees that more will be gained by delivering us out again than by keeping us out altogether. Some of them are our own fault, but some are not. Circumstances sometimes arise that make us feel as if the ground has opened beneath our feet. We do not know where we are, nor what to do. We may find ourselves suddenly in great anxiety or fear or sorrow, or deeply convicted of having sinned—the 'crevasse' of sin is one we all too often fall into—and we may be almost ready to despair. If at such times we have no ground for hope we are indeed in a sad plight.

The Word of God speaks of those who are "*separate from Christ . . . having no hope . . .*" (Eph. 2. 12), and it speaks of others who "abound in hope" because they have "*joy and peace in believing*" (Rom. 15. 13). These latter are the people who, when they fall, know that they are safely united to a 'sledge' that will hold them fast. They are true Christians.

A true Christian is not a person who merely believes certain truths or does (or does not do) certain things. He is one who "*is joined unto the Lord, one spirit*" (I. Cor. 6. 17). The Word of God says, "*Believe on the Lord Jesus, and thou shalt be saved*" (Acts 16. 31); and when we do truly believe on Him, not only are our sins forgiven but the very life of the Lord Jesus is given to us and we become *"partakers of the divine nature"* (II. Peter 1. 4)—united to Him *by His own life.*

This is what the New Testament means when it speaks of people being "in Christ." Such people cannot be separated from Him unless that link of life can be broken; and that can never be, for there is no power—not even death itself—strong enough to overcome the power of His life. When He died on the Cross and rose again from the dead, He overcame all the power of evil, making Himself Master of sin, death and Satan. Paul says in Romans 8. 38,39:

"I am persuaded that neither death, nor life, nor angels . . . nor things present, nor things to come . . . nor height, nor depth, nor any other *creature, shall be able to separate us from the love of God, which is in Christ Jesus our Lord."*

So you see how confident a Christian should be, that even if he falls into difficulty or danger, or even into sin, he can never really be separated from his Saviour, and his hope of deliverance lies not in his own strength, but in the fact that he is united to the Lord Jesus by a bond that nothing can break. And, moreover—unlike the sledge which *might* have fallen down the crevasse—the Lord Jesus is as firm as a rock, established for ever in a place of victory from which He will never be moved. If only we could remember these things when we are in the midst of our trials how much more calmly and triumphantly we should bear the trials.

Paul and Silas remembered them when they fell into a very big 'crevasse' at Philippi. You can read the story in Acts 16. They were in very great trouble. Everything seemed suddenly to have gone wrong. It looked as if the Lord had forsaken them, as if there was no possible way of escape and no ground for hope. What an occasion for despair! They might well have been gloomy and afraid—as I think many of us would have been. But what did they do?

In the black darkness they showed no sign of worry, but prayed and sang hymns to God!

They remembered that, although they had fallen into a deep 'crevasse' that seemed as if it would swallow them up alive, there was a life-line—invisible but very real—that united them to One above, and that so long as that union remained all must be well. Their Lord was livingly joined to them in their trial and what could their enemies do against *Him?* They knew *by faith*—not by sight—that, whatever the appearance of things might be, they had not been abandoned and their Lord would somehow make all the evil circumstances to work out for good. And so instead of despairing they sang in hope; instead of fretting and fearing they rested and quietly waited.

What a deliverance they had in their hearts before ever their bodies were released from prison! And what a great deal of blessing came to others at the time, and has since come to very many more who have read the story, because Paul and Silas fell into that 'crevasse'! We are all glad that God let them go into it, instead of keeping them out of it altogether.

In contrast to Paul and Silas, the disciples of Jesus acted very differently one day when they suddenly fell into a 'crevasse.' They were with Jesus Himself in a boat on the Sea of Galilee, when suddenly a great storm arose and it looked as if the boat would be swamped. The disciples were greatly afraid and expected every moment to be the last for them and for their Master. They had not yet learned that there was no need to be fearful when He was with them.

He Himself was quite at rest. He arose and commanded the wind and the sea to be still, and there was a great calm. Then He said to the astonished disciples, "*Why are ye fearful? Have ye not yet faith?*" (Mark 4. 35-41). What unnecessary fears they had endured! How much better it is to count on the Lord than to fly into a panic!

Do you see what to do when *you* fall into a 'crevasse'?

If you really belong to the Lord Jesus you are *not* abandoned and alone, a poor victim to be overcome and destroyed. You may feel like that, and everything may appear like it, but you must look by faith at the things not seen. You are joined to the Lord Jesus. His life is yours. By the unbreakable power of that life He upholds you. Nothing can separate you from Him. And the end of the story cannot be disaster if He is involved in it.

Count on Him continually. Do it day after day. Even though circumstances do not quickly appear to improve, keep on counting on Him, and overcome the tendency to despair by the assurance that He is Lord of all and therefore all things must in the end yield to Him.

And, as you continue to do this, a strange thing will be happening, which may perhaps take you by surprise: you will suddenly find that, though your circumstances may not have altered, you are no longer feeling as if you are in a 'crevasse.' In heart you will have escaped from it on to firm ground again. You will not have had to call others to your help, as our explorers did, nor will you have saved yourself by frantic struggles.

You will have come up and out as the result of your faith, and the Lord would say to you as He said to others when He was here on the earth—"Thy faith hath saved thee."

Now are you quite sure you are "joined unto the Lord"?

If not, make certain of it now, by believing on Him with all your heart. And then count on Him in every situation, whatever happens, knowing that as long as He lives and triumphs you live and may triumph too in the power of His life. The boy or girl who most counts on Him in times of difficulty and trial—who lays hold most firmly on eternal life—will be the first to reach the 'South Pole.'

Count on Him, count on Him,
Every hour of every day:
Count on Him, count on Him!
He says you may.
Jesus triumphant all along the line;
Triumphant Saviour, all Thy triumph mine;
For since I am a partner in Thy love,
My life on earth is lived through thee above.

Chapter Nine

THE WORST JOURNEY IN THE WORLD

WOULD YOU HAVE GONE ON OR TURNED BACK?

"Love . . . endureth all things" (1. Cor. 13. 7).

"Jesus . . . endured . . ." (Heb. 12. 2).

"Jesus, having loved his own which were in the world, he loved them unto the end" (John 13. 1).

UNTIL the time of our story no actual exploring had ever been done in the Antarctic during the winter. At that season the sun disappears altogether for four months, during which there is the darkness of night, broken only by the moon and stars. And with the darkness is the cold—so severe that we in England can form no idea of it. Everything is frozen as hard as rock, and death from exposure would be very easy. The explorers remain as much as possible in their hut, where they have light and warmth, and nobody goes outdoors except for really important reasons.

But there was one special piece of work to be done by Capt. Scott's party which could only be done in the winter, and which involved a journey to a point seventy miles away. Some considered it madness to attempt such a journey, but those concerned thought it worth trying, in spite of the risks; and so three men set out. No one knew what conditions would have to be faced, nor what dangers would be encountered. The route they would have to follow lay over a part of the country they knew very little about, except that it was covered with great ridges of ice like huge waves of a frozen sea, over or along which they would have to make their way. And those frozen waves were likely to be full of crevasses into which the men could very easily fall. All this had to be faced in darkness, and in such cold as no man had ever before endured. It was not an inviting prospect. One of the three men who went—the writer of the book from which our stories are taken—called it afterwards 'the worst journey in the world.'

As the travellers stepped out into the bitter darkness and set forth, pulling their heavy sledges behind them, the comfort and light and warmth of the hut, and the companionship of the men they were leaving there, must have seemed very attractive. Our writer admits that he felt a little frightened. All of them in their hearts must have felt they dared not look back or they would have been sorely tempted to return. They had to set their faces like a flint and press steadily forward.

Six weeks passed before they returned in safety to the hut. We can have only a very small idea of what they suffered in those weeks. The story of it sounds almost impossible to believe. It scarcely makes any impression on us to read that at times the temperature was more than 100 degrees below freezing point. In England we think it terribly cold when it is only 10 degrees below! The writer of our book says:

Those days were, I suppose, in their dark severity the worst that men have ever come through alive. . . The horror of them would have to be experienced to be appreciated . . . it is not possible to describe it.'

The men would pull for hours at their sledges, keeping more or less warm by the exercise. As soon as they stopped, they would begin to freeze. Their clothing often froze into solid sheets that would not bend. At rest times they would pitch their tent—a very cold and painful task—and then, having with great difficulty made a hot meal, they would try to get into their sleeping bags. They would find the bags frozen into solid blocks which would take perhaps an hour to thaw out. Then they would creep inside, only to find the bags thickly coated with ice which gradually melted owing to the warmth of their bodies, and the men had to lie there wet and shivering! After their hours of so-called rest, they would get up, thankful that the ordeal was over, and their wet sleeping bags would in a few minutes be frozen again into solid blocks of ice, requiring to be thawed out again at the next resting place. And to these discomforts were added difficulties and dangers too many to describe here.

Our writer says the cold was bad enough, but that it was the perpetual darkness that added horror to it. They could never be sure what lay before them. Often they misjudged things and distances and found themselves in trouble trying to haul their sledges up and down and out of the maze of great frozen waves that surrounded them on all sides. The astonishing thing is that men could go on in such circumstances. It would have been easier to return to the hut and explain how impossible it was to finish the journey. No one would have doubted them or called them cowards. They would have been counted heroes for even setting out at all. But had they yielded to the temptation to return *they would never have accomplished the task which they set out to perform.*

I have not told you what that task was—I will keep that for another time, and it will surprise you when you know it—but, whatever it was, it would have been left undone. That might not have mattered very much in this case; but suppose it had been very important indeed, something that simply must be done or else terrible consequences would follow. In that case, no matter how difficult the way, how great the dangers, how fierce the cold, how deep the darkness, how terrible the sufferings, they *must* go on. Well, all honour to our three explorers—they went on and succeeded.

But I want to use the rest of my space in writing of One Who accomplished a journey much worse than 'the worst journey in the world'—and Who did it, not with the helpful companionship of others who shared His sufferings, but alone. Had He failed, heaven would have remained closed to us all, and everlasting separation from God would have been our fate. Oh, thank God that He did not fail!

Before coming to this world as a babe at Bethlehem, our Lord Jesus Christ, the Son of God, had been "*with God . . . in the bosom of the Father*" (John 1. 1. 18). There He had enjoyed the warmth of perfect love in an atmosphere of utter purity and light, for "*God is light, and in him is no darkness at all*" (I. John 1. 5). But when He came into this world everything was different for Him. He lived His life of perfect holiness and love, but He was surrounded on every side by sin and hatred and darkness. *"Men loved the darkness rather than the light; for their works were evil"* (John 3. 19).

Enemies were constantly at work against Him. Satan was continually tempting Him, in an effort either to destroy Him, --or to ruin His work. He loved others, but few loved Him in return; and even of those few, most of them completely misunderstood Him, and scarcely one could enter at all deeply into what He felt and thought; and in the hour of His greatest need not even one was found standing with Him. If only, sometimes, there had been one with whom He could share His burden! But there was not one. How bitterly cold and dark this world was for Him! He was truly "*despised and rejected of men; a man of sorrows and acquainted with grief*" (Isaiah 53.3).

And from the very beginning He knew that the worst suffering of all lay at the end of the journey—the Cross on which He was to die. Yet He went forward, never looking back. Such courage and self-sacrifice puts to shame the noblest and bravest act of other men, and no other human suffering can be compared with it. No one but the Son of God could have borne what He bore, not only on the Cross, but through the years that led up to it.

And why did He endure so much? It was for love's sake.

The only way that sinful men could be saved was by a sinless Man bearing the judgment of God on their behalf—and the death of the Cross was the way God had appointed for this. 'There was no other good enough to pay the price of sin'—only the Son of God; and for this purpose, He came and lived in this world. But even He had to be *proved* sinless; and therefore He had to be tempted and tried at all points, and tested along every line of human suffering.

Through all the years of His life here, the great question that was involved was this—would He go right through to the end? Would His love for His Father's will and for sinful men stand the tremendous strain, or would He take the easier way and return to heaven without finishing the work He had come to do?

We shall never cease to praise Him that He bore it all and endured—"*having loved his own which were in the world, he loved them unto the end*" (John 13.1). Almost the last cry on His lips upon the Cross before He died was a loud one. "*It is finished!*" (John 19. 30). And this really meant 'Victory!' It was the triumph of His love over every evil thing; and it was the outcome of the worst journey that was ever undertaken.

The measure of His love for us is shown by the measure of His sufferings for us. I can say, with Paul, that He "*loved me, and gave himself up for me*" (Gal. 2. 20).

Can you say it also?

If so, will you pray that day by day you may understand better what that love cost Him, and that you may love Him more and more in return? I am quite sure that the boy or girl who loves Him most will make the greatest progress in knowing Him, and will be the first to reach the 'South Pole' of the land we are exploring.

He did it for me, He did it for me,
A sinner as guilty as ever could be;
Oh, how I love Him, now that I see
He suffered, He died, and He did it for me.

Chapter Ten

WONDERFUL ESCAPES

CAN YOU FIND ANY REASON FOR BOASTING?

"God . . . is rich in mercy . . ." (Eph. 2.4).

"I trust in the mercy of God for ever and ever" (Psa. 52. 8).

WE must continue the story of the three explorers who set out in the depth of winter on 'the worst journey in the world.' I told you last time of some of their difficulties and dangers. Yet they pressed on, completed their task and returned safely to their companions, who received them with every possible honour. As we read the story, we must feel that no honour could be too great for men who could suffer and endure, and triumph in spite of so much. If the three men had boasted of their great achievement, we could not be surprised. But the truth is that there were occasions in their journey when all their wonderful courage and powers of endurance would have been utterly useless if God had not miraculously saved them. How many times they were saved from unseen dangers, neither they nor we can ever know, but we read of two occasions on which quite clearly only the mercy of God delivered them from certain death.

The first incident concerned one of those constant enemies of our explorers—a crevasse. The men were journeying down a slope, pulling their sledge behind them, in the darkness of the night. Clouds had covered the moon for many hours, so that they had little or no benefit from her light. Quite suddenly the clouds parted in front of the moon and her light shone out clearly; and in that moment the men saw, only three paces in front of them, a great crevasse into which they were just about to step. If they had gone in, the sledge would certainly have followed them down, and there would have been no possibility whatever of their escape.

All their courage and skill could not have helped them.

It was the rolling away of the clouds from the face of the moon that saved them.

And who did that?

I am glad that the writer of our book acknowledges that they owed their deliverance to God alone. Truly they might have said, "*Not by works . . .which we did ourselves, but according to his mercy he saved us*" (Titus 3. 5).

The second incident was even more remarkable. It concerned their tent. We must remember that the cold was so great that if the men stood still in the open for even a few minutes they were in danger of being frozen to death, and therefore it was of the utmost importance that they should have shelter and warmth when they rested. The only possible way of providing this was by erecting their little tent every time they halted. It protected them from the wind and snow, and, with the help of an oil stove, enabled them to enjoy a little warmth. To have been without their tent even for a few hours would certainly have meant death for the explorers. Their very life was bound up with it.

After three weeks of indescribable hardship, they at last reached the place for which they had set out. It was on the rocky slope of a mountain. They had planned on arrival to build themselves a shelter out of the rocks, so that they could live more comfortably for the few days that they must remain there. This they did—with much difficulty—but it was not a very great success, and so they pitched their tent nearby in a sheltered place and stored most of their goods in it.

All went well for a day or two, and after a heavy day's work they lay down to rest. The weather was calm, with absolute silence outside. Then there came a sob of wind, and all was calm again. Ten minutes later, and the wind was blowing as if the world had gone mad. The earth seemed to be torn in pieces; the fury and roar of it cannot be imagined or described. The shelter itself, though built of rocks, threatened to collapse. Almost immediately one of the men cried out, 'The tent has gone!' It was nowhere to be seen.

Although it had been very firmly pitched and well secured to the ground, the terrible force of the wind had carried it away as if it had been a piece of paper. In such a hurricane, it would be blown miles away in a few minutes, and in any case, it was impossible in such conditions to go and look for it. The explorers could do nothing but lie in their sleeping bags in their shelter and wait for the wind to drop. Part of the hut collapsed on them. They had no food. They dare not move outside. For two whole days and nights the hurricane continued.

Then conditions improved enough to allow the men to go outside. They knew it was hopeless to look for the tent, but because their life depended on their finding it, they decided to search. Such a wind as had been blowing for forty-eight hours must have carried the tent, like a parachute, hundreds of miles away. And, remember, it was winter and quite dark all the time. What was the use of looking for the tent at all in such circumstances? But they started out—and half a mile away they found it, lying in a sheltered hollow and almost undamaged!

Our writer says: *'Our lives had been taken away and given back to us. We were so thankful, we said nothing.'*

Could the explorers claim any credit for their deliverance?

No, it was God's doing. Once more the only suitable language to describe the truth of the matter could be, "*Not by works . . . which we did ourselves, but according to his mercy he saved us.*"

Now our explorers were engaged in a very earthly enterprise. It had nothing to do with what we call the work of God. But that does not affect the lesson we can learn from their story. The mercy of God concerns us all, and in all circumstances. Everyone, from time to time, has occasion to exclaim, 'What a mercy that *that* happened (or, that so and so did *not* happen) *just then*!' In most cases it is quite clear that nobody but a loving, all-seeing, all-powerful God had any part in causing matters to fall out as they did.

It is one of the chief delights of true Christians to notice how frequently God does thus act to save them. It is also one of their chief wonders—for why should a holy God be so gracious towards sinful people?

We all have sinned: there is none righteous, no, not one. Yet in His great mercy, God sent His Son, the Lord Jesus Christ, into the world, that the world through Him might be saved; and men committed the greatest sin of all by crucifying Him.

Could we reasonably expect that God would continue to shew mercy to such a people?

But herein lies the greatest of all mercies—for in the very death that He died, the Son of God took upon Himself the sin of the world and bore the judgment of God on our behalf; and because of that sacrifice God has been able to be merciful towards sinners. He will shew His mercy towards every one of us in many ways until we finally and deliberately refuse to acknowledge His love—and then mercy will have to give place to judgment.

I must be careful to emphasize one thing.

Although I have said that it was only the mercy of God, and not the skill of the explorers, that enabled them to succeed in their task, I want you to notice also that they would never have succeeded if they themselves had been careless or lazy or timid. They had to do their utmost, and to bear bravely all the hardships and sufferings involved. God requires this of us in all that we do.

His word tells us, *"Whatsoever thy hand findeth to do, do it with thy might"* (Ecc. 9. 10) and *"Whatsoever ye do, work heartily as unto the Lord"* (Col. 3. 23).

Carelessness and laziness can never be excused in those who call themselves Christians. But the great lesson that we have to learn is this—that although we do all we can do, we *always* need the mercy of God.

No man was ever more capable, or worked harder or suffered more for the sake of the gospel, than the apostle Paul. If any man could have succeeded by his own labours, Paul ought to have done so. But it was he who wrote, *"Not that we are sufficient of ourselves . . . our sufficiency is from God"* (II Cor. 3. 5). And he went further than that; he wrote, *"We despaired. . . that we should not trust in ourselves, but in God . . ."* (II. Cor. 1. 8, 9).

Some of the things which he suffered were deliberately allowed by God in order to make him know that if God withheld His mercy even for a moment, Paul himself would be without hope and all his labour in vain. This is not an easy lesson for anyone to learn, but we all need to learn it.

In all of us there is pride that makes us think that we can do things for God, and we have to be brought to an end of ourselves in order that we may trust wholly in God and not in ourselves. This involves deeper things than I propose to speak of now.

For the present, we will be content with this one thing—that we need the mercy of God always and in every situation; and the happiest and most blessed people, and those most fruitful in God's service, are they who know most deeply their dependence upon Him Who *"delighteth in mercy"* (Micah 7. 18). He will certainly not withhold His mercy from any one who trusts in Him. *"The eye of the Lord is upon them that fear him, upon them that hope in his mercy; to deliver their soul from death and to keep them alive in famine"* (Psa. 33. 18, 19).

David delighted to speak of God as *"the God of my mercy"* (Ps. 59. 10).

Have you found Him to be also the God of *your* mercy?

I suggest that you kneel down and ask that He will make you like David who said, "I trust in the mercy of God for ever and ever."

In the spiritual land which we are exploring together, the boy or girl who will first reach the 'South Pole' is the one who, while doing his or her utmost and doing everything "heartily as unto the Lord" yet at the same time trusts most fully in the mercy of God—mercy which is "*from everlasting to everlasting upon them that fear him*" (Ps. 103. 17).

For His love floweth on, free and full as a river;
And His mercy endureth for ever and ever.

Chapter Eleven

BIRDS'-NESTING UNDER DIFFICULTIES

ARE YOU LOOKING FOR 'EGGS'?

Jesus said "... love one another, even as I have loved you" (John 15. 12).

"The love of Christ constraineth us" (II. Cor. 5. 14).
"... that I may by any means save some" (I. Cor. 9.22).

I KNOW you are wondering what was the reason which led our explorers to endure so many hardships and dangers on 'the worst journey in the world.' Well, it is time I told you. They were going birds'-nesting! They were looking for birds' eggs! You find it hard to believe, but it is true. Let me explain.

Scientists had certain theories about the origin of birds, and they hoped that if they could examine the eggs of a certain bird called the Emperor Penguin, they would be able to prove their theories. This particular bird lives only in the Antarctic region, and nobody had ever found any of its eggs. Some years before our story, Capt. Scott had been to the Antarctic and had found a large number of the birds living on the ice in a certain bay. It was springtime—the season when most birds lay their eggs—but in this case all the eggs had already been hatched and only young birds, not eggs, were found. From this it was concluded that these birds must lay during the winter season, and that if any eggs were to be obtained someone must go in the bitter cold and darkness of winter to find them. That is what our explorers were doing.

I have told you something of their sufferings and adventures on their journey. They eventually arrived in the neighborhood where the penguins lived. Then some of their worst troubles began. It was necessary for the men to get down to the ice on the seashore at the foot of high, ice-covered cliffs. They made one attempt and failed. The next day they tried again and succeeded. There they found a number of the birds, some of them with eggs. They collected five eggs—as many as they could take with them on their perilous journey—but broke two of them on their way back up the cliffs. What precious things the three remaining eggs were! No gold could have bought them—only the sufferings and endurance of the explorers could have obtained them. You would expect that those eggs would be amongst the most treasured things in the world today. Well, they were eventually brought home to England and examined by expert scientists, with results which were rather disappointing to the scientists. What they had hoped to find they did not find. I do not know what has become of the eggs—most likely they were thrown away long ago or, at best, they may have been preserved in a museum somewhere as objects of interest for the few people who care to look at them. We should honour very highly the men who acted so courageously in the cause to which they had given themselves; but, apart from the magnificent example which they set us, I wonder whether the world is really any better off today than it was before, in spite of the suffering endured in finding the eggs. We are bound to ask the question –was it worthwhile?

All that I can say is that I should be very sorry to pay so great a price for so little result. It reminds us of the melancholy words of one who said, "*Then I looked on all the works that my hands had wrought, and on the labour that I had laboured to do; and, behold, all was vanity and a striving after wind, and there was no profit. . .*" (Eccles. 2. 11).

What a tragedy if, after labouring and suffering, anyone has to make such a confession!

We need to be sure that our lives are devoted to that which is profitable, and the only way to ensure that is to ask God to keep us in the way of His will—not our own will or the will of other people—doing always those things which are well-pleasing *to Him.* What *is* His will? What *is* worth doing? Many answers might be given, but I am going to give only one of them here.

You will remember that in one of our talks together we spoke of the Lord Jesus Christ and the costly road that He travelled for our sakes. He counted no suffering too great, and endured even the death of the Cross in order to save us from our sins, because He loved us. What He accomplished by His death and resurrection was great enough to save *everybody,* but people could not enter into the benefit of what He had done for them unless they knew about it—and they could not know unless they were told. And so almost the last words that He spoke to His disciples before He went back to heaven were these: "*All authority hath been given unto me in heaven and on earth. Go ye therefore, and make disciples of all the nations. . . and lo, I am with you alway*" (Matt. 28. 18, 19).

He needed His disciples to tell others about Him, but He promised that He Himself would be with them all the time, though unseen—ready at every moment to work for them if they trusted Him; to guide them to the right people, to give them wisdom, to strengthen them to bear all the trials encountered, and to overcome all the power of evil that rose up against them. Ever since then, men and women who love Him have been telling others the good news, seeking to win hearts to Him. Many of God's faithful servants have left their homes and loved ones in order to go forth to distant places to make known what the Lord Jesus has done for men.

I expect you have read the life stories of some missionaries and will know how greatly some of them suffered—many of them even unto death. Others suffered in less obvious ways—in having to live among people of evil and unclean habits, to endure patiently the foolishness of ignorant people, to bear cheerfully the loss of their possessions, and very often to be misunderstood and misjudged by the very people whom they sought to help.

Why did they go into such conditions? Why did they not turn back and give it all up when they found how difficult the way was?

The answer is that the love of God Himself was in their hearts, and they had come to share His desire for those who so greatly needed what He only could give them. His love reaches to every single one in all the world, for it is His will "*That all men should be saved, and come to the knowledge of the truth*" (I. Tim. 2. 4).

You remember the Lord Jesus often spoke about sheep. On one occasion, speaking of Himself as He were a shepherd with some of His sheep gathered safely around Him. He said, "*Other sheep I have . . . them also I must bring*" (John 10. 16); and in the parable of the lost sheep He likened Himself to the shepherd who leaves all the rest of the flock and goes after that which is lost, "*until he find it*" (Luke 15. 4).

What a great deal is contained in that word 'until'!

Patience, endurance, perseverance, courage, longing, suffering—who can tell how much may be involved? And all this is explained by one fact—the heavenly Shepherd loves His sheep.

And it is He Who says to those who love Him, "*Go ye into all the world and preach the gospel*" (Mark 16. 15).

If we change the thought from sheep to eggs, in order to fit in with the story of our explorers, it is as if He said, 'There are some eggs that I very specially want to be found and brought to me. I want you to go and find them.'

If you and I know that He is saying that to us, and if we are to succeed as the explorers did, then we must be ready to endure as they endured, and to pay the price of success. The difficulties we shall encounter may not be physical ones like cold and darkness, cliffs and crevasses, storms and blizzards—though many of God's servants are meeting exactly that kind of trial in their work—but we shall certainly meet the equally real difficulties of cold hearts, darkened minds, steep descents into places of humbling and ridicule, all kinds of pitfalls into which Satan tries to make us fall, and the howling winds and blinding blizzards of doubt and discouragement.

Shall we give up because of them, or keep on until we find that which we seek?

I fear most of us will give up very quickly unless we love as the Lord Jesus loved; and the only way we can do that is by having His own love shed abroad in our hearts—loving others with the same love with which He loves us and them. The very nature of that love makes it to desire the salvation of others, and so it will stir us up to seek them, to lead them to Christ. It will make us willing even to suffer ourselves if only they can be brought to Him. It will give us strength far beyond our own, and enable us to continue when we should otherwise give up. His love is the greatest power in all this world—and we may have it working in our hearts if we will.

Have you yet started on this kind of 'bird's-nesting'?

It is certainly work worth doing, and not at all like "vanity and a striving after wind." It will bring joy to the hearts of all concerned—including God Himself—and the results will last for ever and ever. The 'eggs' to be sought are the lives of others whom the Lord longs to have for Himself. Will you ask Him to teach you how to do this work?

The first thing to ask is that He will fill you with His own love. All else will follow after that. There are many 'eggs' quite near to us—the people we live with, or whom we meet every day—and we must begin by seeking them; but God may want some of us to go to those who are further away. Are you willing to go if He calls you? Will you hold back because of the difficulties, or turn back when once you have started? Or will you trust Him to take you triumphantly through to the end? I should like to think that as you read these words, you will hear His voice saying to you "*Whom shall I send, and who will go for us?*" Will you answer, "*Here am I: send me*"? (Isaiah 6.6, 8)

I think it will be found that the one whose heart is most filled with the love of God and who most willingly 'lays down his life' in seeking others for the Lord Jesus will be first to reach the 'South Pole' of the land we are exploring. May the Lord make us all very keen and capable at 'bird's-nesting'!

Lord, lay some soul upon my heart,
And love that soul through me;
And may I humbly do my part
To win that soul for Thee.

Chapter Twelve

PENGUINS

ARE YOU AS WISE AS AN 'EMPEROR'?

"God gave unto us eternal life, and this life is in his Son.
He that hath the Son hath the life;
he that hath not the Son of God
hath not the life" (I. John 5. 11, 12).

IN our last story we were speaking about the eggs of the bird called the Emperor Penguin. I think you will be interested to know a little more about the habits of this bird and how she cares for her eggs.

I expect most of you have either seen a live penguin or a picture of one, but probably this was the more common variety of penguin, a little fellow with a blue-black coat and a white shirt-front, whose average weight is about 16 pounds. But the Emperor is a great, dignified person with long curved beak and bright orange headwear, and weighs about 6 ½ stone—as much as a healthy boy of about 13 years old. She does not sit upon her eggs, as most other birds do. She can care for only one egg at a time, and this she 'nurses,' resting the egg upon her feet and pressing it closely to a patch of bare skin in the lower part of her body.

You will remember that I told you the eggs are laid in mid-winter, in the coldest and bleakest conditions known anywhere on earth, and it is not surprising that many of the eggs or the young chicks perish. Not more than about one egg out of every four laid produces a chick that comes to full growth. And because so many parents lose their eggs, they are always eagerly looking around to try and steal one from another bird; and so a continual campaign goes on throughout the colony where they live. Even the most careful parent must go down to the water's edge from time to time to search for food, and in doing so she may have to leave her egg unattended.

The moment she moves, a dozen other penguins nearby are ready to pounce on the egg and seize it for themselves, and, when the real parent returns, the egg is gone—either broken in the fight or captured by another owner. Most of the parent birds have to be content in the end to have no egg and no chick. But many of them try to get over the disappointment in a curious way—they nurse a lump of ice instead, shaped roughly like a proper egg and about the same size! Our explorers saw one bird drop an ice egg, which was immediately seized by another bird, but forsaken later on when a real egg became available. It looks therefore as if the birds know the difference between a real egg and a false one.

And so, in that desolate spot the fight for existence goes on, and the parent birds hopefully try to hatch chicks out of lumps of ice. What a pitiful story it is – expending labour and love wholly in vain! You may laugh at the foolishness of it—but be quite sure that you are not doing the same thing!

You know, of course, what is the all-important difference between a true egg and an ice egg. An ice egg may look very much like a real one on the outside. The penguin may treat it just like a real one; she may think or pretend that she is doing some good by nursing it; but nothing that she or anyone else can do will ever alter the fact that it is only a lump of dead ice, and a living chick cannot come out of that.

But how different is the real egg!

In it is life, and, if properly cared for, that life will grow and develop, and in due course be seen as a living chick which, all being well, will become a full-grown Emperor.

It is the presence of life that makes all the difference.

Now this matter of life is of tremendous importance in the things of God. It is a great mistake to think that everybody walking about in the world today is 'alive.' They are 'alive' *to us*, but not necessarily *to God.*

The first people whom God created, Adam and Eve, were 'alive' to Him; He could walk with them and talk with them (Gen. 3. 8), and take delight in them (Gen 1. 28, 31). But when they sinned (as you can read in Gen. 3.) they 'died' to God—that is, although their bodies did not immediately become dead in the sense in which we understand that word, a great separation in spirit came between themselves and God, and man became a 'fallen,' sinful, changed being in whom there remained no good thing.

This does not mean that God ceased to love and to care for man, but it does mean that He could now receive nothing from man which could be acceptable to Him. And everyone since born of Adam's race has been born "*dead in trespasses and sins*" (Eph. 2.1), and no matter what anyone may do and however hard he may try, he is 'dead' to God and that is the end of the matter. He is like an ice egg, that can never produce anything. There is nothing possible for God under those conditions.

But, thank God, there is a way of hope. There was one Person—Jesus Christ—born into this world Who, though very much like all others on the outside, was nevertheless quite different inwardly. It soon became evident that there was a nature and a power in Him that was not in any other person on earth. His touch, His words, His life, accomplished things which no others could do.

He explained the difference in this way—"*Ye have not life in yourselves*" (John 6. 53); "*I am the resurrection and the life*" (John 11. 25); "*I am the Living one*" (Rev. 1. 18); "*The words that I have spoken unto you are spirit, and are life*" (John 6.63). "*In him was life*" (John 1. 4)—not simply the life of man but the life of God Himself. This is what the Bible calls 'eternal life.' *In the midst of a world full of people, He was the only One Who was really 'alive.'*

The secret was that He was the sinless Son of God, who had come forth from God in order to make a way whereby other people, who were 'dead' to God, might be enabled to share His life and thus become 'alive' to God. The one way to this was by the offering up of that holy life of His upon the Cross as a sacrifice for the sins of men. Then in His resurrection He took up that life again, and, having gone back to heaven, He sent forth the Holy Spirit to bring that life into men who saw their need and were ready to receive Him. Ever since then, countless multitudes of 'dead' people have been "born from above" by receiving into their hearts the Spirit of the Living One Himself, and thus His words have been fulfilled, "*I came that they may have life, and may have it abundantly*" (John 10. 10).

These "born from above" ones are no longer like ice eggs but like real eggs—they now have the life of God within them, and if that life is allowed to have its way and to develop, there will come forth something which bears the very features of Jesus Christ Himself, and God will have that in which He can rejoice.

I want to ask you very seriously—are you like an ice egg or a real egg?

Here is the way of knowing: *"He that hath the Son hath the life; he that hath not the Son of God hath not the life"* (I. John 5. 12).

But we must go further. You will see that, with God, life is not just a 'thing'—it is a Person: it is His Son. No one can have life without having the Son. And if what we do for God is to have any value in His sight, it must in some way be the expression of that Son; otherwise all that we do will be only like nursing an ice egg—it will bring forth nothing for God.

There is any amount of so-called Christian work today which looks like the real thing, but it is not. Much effort and enthusiasm and sacrifice—many meetings—much saying of prayers and listening to addresses – trying to be good, trying to be religious—and yet it may all be dead. *"Dead works"* the Bible calls those painful efforts and duties (Heb. 6. 1).

Why are they dead?

Because, for some reason or other, Jesus Christ the Living One is not in them.

Bring Him into them, and what a difference there will be! Instead of merely trying to do your best for God, open your heart anew to His Son, and ask Him to live His own life, and do His own work through you. Instead of trying to say prayers, ask Him to put

His own desires into your heart—then prayer will become alive! Instead of reading the Bible as weary drudgery, ask that Jesus Christ may be in you as the power to understand, and that you may find Him in every page and you will be amazed how even the 'dry' parts—like "Leviticus" and "Proverbs" – become wonderfully alive and full of helpfulness.

Even your daily tasks—let the Living One into every part of your life and you will be astonished what a difference it will make!

Everything will live!

And not only so—you will be able to do things you could never do before, for *He* will do them through you and there is nothing too hard for Him.

The one great rule of Paul's life was this—"*to me to live is Christ*" (Phil. 1.21). That means that he had no interest in anything in which Jesus Christ had no part. He did not waste his time in any work that Jesus Christ did not give him to do. He did not make his own plans and then ask God to bless them. He had this understanding with the Lord—that the Lord should take complete charge of every part of him and should live His own life through Paul, choosing for him where he should go and what he should do. This resulted often in suffering and difficulty for Paul, but his attitude was – 'I want every part of my life to bring forth something for God's pleasure, and therefore, whatever it costs me, I want the living Lord to live His life in me.' Paul had no time to waste trying to hatch out ice eggs! For him, it was Jesus Christ or nothing.

Alas, many a man has spent his life in so-called Christian work, and at the end it will be found to have been mostly "dead works" because Jesus Christ was not really the centre and life of most of it; and all his good intentions will not have made any difference to the result. Everything will be determined by whether the Living One was in it or not.

Now may I ask, how it is with you?

If you look into your own life, at all the things you are doing, do you see any ice eggs that have no life in them and therefore can never produce anything for God? Are there any parts of your life from which the Living One is shut out?

If so, why go on like that?

Get rid of the ice eggs! Change them for real eggs! Even a rather stupid 'Emperor' seemed to know the difference between the two and chose a real egg when she had the chance. Are you not as wise as a penguin?

I should like to encourage you with one final word. A penguin's egg, when hatched, produces a penguin; and in just the same way, the life of Jesus, when developed, reproduces the nature of Jesus. The young penguins, you remember, are hatched out in the coldest place on earth, and, though many die, some of them overcome and live.

The living Lord Jesus has already overcome every enemy and every trial that can ever come to Him, and now not even death itself has any dominion over Him. Those in whom He lives can also be "*more than conquerors through him that loved us*" (Rom. 8. 37). He can make them "overcomers." And that is better even than being an 'Emperor'!

Are you one? You can be, if you know Jesus Christ as your very life. Let His life have free scope in you, and everything that God wills for you becomes possible.

The boy or girl who can most truly say "to me to live is Christ" will certainly be the first to reach the 'South Pole.'

I give my heart to Thee,
Thy dwelling-place to be;
I want Thee ever in my heart,
O, live Thy life in me.

Chapter Thirteen

FROZEN IN

HAVE YOU ANY DYNAMITE?

"Power belongeth unto God" (Psalm 62. 11).

"Thanks be to God, which giveth us the victory through our Lord Jesus Christ" (I. Cor. 15.57).

ONE of the most thrilling incidents recorded in our book concerns Capt. Scott's ship the 'Discovery' which he used on his first visit to the Antarctic. At one period the sea in which the ship was anchored became frozen and continued so for many months, so that the 'Discovery' remained there, fixed immovably in very thick ice. It was expected that with the return of warmer weather the ice would break up and the ship would be set free, but for some unexplained reason this did not happen, and the ship remained imprisoned. This continued for so long that the position of the whole expedition became very serious. Everything was attempted that offered any hope of release. Twenty miles of ice lay between the ship and the open sea. A vain attempt was made to saw a channel from a half-way point. Explosions in the ice were tried, but with no result. The explorers almost despaired of freedom. But one day there came a change in the situation. A shout from one of the men brought all the rest racing from their hut to the slopes above the bay where the ship was lying. This is how Capt. Scott described the scene:

'The ice was breaking up right across the Strait, and with a rapidity which we had not thought possible. No sooner was one great ice floe borne away than a dark streak cut its way into the solid sheet that remained, and carved out another, to feed the broad stream of pack-ice which was hurrying away towards the open sea. I have never witnessed a more impressive sight. The wind had fallen to a dead calm, and not a sound disturbed the peaceful stillness about us. Yet in the midst of this peaceful silence was an awful, unseen agency rending that great ice-sheet as though it had been naught but the thinnest paper. We knew well by this time the nature of our prison bars; we had not plodded again and again over those long dreary miles of ice and snow without realizing the formidable strength of the great barrier which held us bound; we knew that the heaviest battleship would have shattered itself ineffectually against it, and we had seen a million-ton iceberg brought to rest at its edge. For weeks we had been struggling with this mighty obstacle; but now without a word, without an effort on our part, it was all melting away, and we knew that in an hour or two not a vestige of it would be left and that the open sea would be lapping on the black rocks below us.'

Can you imagine the excitement and the relief? The ship had been like a city besieged by an army. There was no way out until the surrounding ice had been broken. Man's utmost strength proved pitifully unequal to the task; but to the power of God working through nature there was no difficulty at all. "*The things which are impossible with men are possible with God*" (Luke 18. 27).

We often find ourselves in a similar position of difficulty. Our 'ship' becomes frozen in, through circumstances arising which make it impossible for us to do even what we believe God wants us to do. It sometimes seems as if the circumstances have acquired an uncanny wisdom—as if things and events, which in themselves certainly have no power to think and to plan have suddenly become capable of planning and scheming, and are working together with the one purpose of hedging us in so that we cannot move. And that is often truer than we might suppose; there frequently *is* such a plan in operation, and a clever mind and powerful hand at work upon our circumstances, with the very object of hindering us. The mind and hand belong to Satan. He uses events and things in the world to hinder the work of God and to hold in captivity those who seek to serve God. His grip upon a human life is first known when the person concerned seeks to escape from the bondage of sin. How strong are Satan's chains! How great and thick the doors and bars of the prison in which he holds the sinner! How thick and unbreakable is the 'ice'! No amount of human effort can ever set free from such captivity; it will fail as completely as the efforts of the explorers to free their ship. A greater power is needed—and, praise God, it is available through Jesus Christ.

But even when we have found deliverance from the power of sin, we are by no means at the end of these 'besiegings'—rather the contrary. Satan will do his utmost to keep us shut in so that we cannot do the will of God. Our 'ship' is frozen in again and again! Unfortunately, at such times we often fail to understand what is happening, and we set about trying by our own efforts to break the 'ice.'

Perhaps in our case the 'ice' consists of an awkward person who will not allow us to do what we feel God wants us to do, and we try to persuade that person to change his mind—and he will not.

Perhaps some circumstance has arisen that blocks our path, and we try to alter it—and cannot. Perhaps it is some duty that falls to us just at a critical moment and threatens to prevent us from going somewhere that the Lord wants us to go, and we try to put the duty on to someone else—and can find nobody to take it.

Perhaps so common a thing as a change of weather threatens to hinder the work of God; perhaps sickness arises; perhaps we suddenly feel too tired to do what we are sure God wants us to do.

Oh, there may be many different things that 'freeze our ship into the ice' and make it impossible for us to move her.

What are we to do?

Try to saw through the twenty miles of ice? Try to blow holes in it with the poor, weak explosions of our own efforts? We shall make no progress that way.

We need another kind of power altogether—the power of God. You may like to know that in the New Testament (which was written originally in the Greek language) the Greek word used to describe that power is *dunamis,* from which comes our English word 'dynamite.' Far better to have God's dynamite at work than ours!

The Bible contains many stories that show us the power of God in action, breaking in pieces the doors of brass, and cutting in sunder the bars of iron (Isaiah 45. 2). At the Red Sea the children of Israel were shut in between the sea and the Egyptian army, and could do nothing to free themselves. Moses said to them, "*Fear ye not, stand still, and see the salvation of the Lord, which he will work for you today*" (Ex. 14. 13). And by

God's power the waters of the sea were divided and the way of escape made.

At Jerusalem, when Jehoshaphat and his people were threatened by overwhelming hosts of their enemies and had to say, "*we have no might . . .neither know we what to do,*" God's message to them was, "*Ye shall not need to fight. . .stand ye still, and see the salvation of the Lord with you*" (II. Chron. 20. 12, 17); and the mighty power of God destroyed the enemies, and His people were freed.

Again at Jerusalem, when Hezekiah and his people were besieged by the Assyrians and could do nothing to release themselves, they cried to the Lord to deliver them, and His answer was, "*Be not afraid. . . of the king of Assyria. . . He shall return unto his own land . . . for I will defend this city to save it . . .*" (Isaiah 37. 7, 35). And without Hezekiah's army doing anything whatever, without a sound and with the greatest ease, the 'ice' was broken up and disappeared! We read (verse 36), "*The angel of the Lord went forth, and smote in the camps of the Assyrians 185,000. So Sennacherib, king of Assyria, departed. . .*" What a simple solution of an 'impossible' problem! Truly there is nothing too hard for the Lord!

Many years later, Peter was shut up in prison, chained to the soldiers that guarded him. His friends outside longed for his release, but what power had they to break up the 'ice' that held him fast? It was another 'impossible' situation. So they prayed.

And that very night Peter was set free by an angel, the gates of the prison opened of their own accord, and he found himself at liberty. The 'ice' had melted and the 'ship' was released, and nobody but God had done anything—except by prayer! (Acts 12. 1-19). How easy for God, but how impossible for men!

Now let us specially note some matters.

I. How does God show His power?

Generally, in a way that does not appear very wonderful or sensational. Things 'just happen.' The awkward person may simply change his mind; the difficult circumstance may just disappear; some unexpected friend may turn up just at the critical moment and relieve us of that awkward duty; the threatened change of weather may not take place; the sickness may pass; our tiredness may just be forgotten. Nothing very sensational about any of these things—but our own efforts could not accomplish them. They represent the operation of the mighty power of God. Without a sound, without effort, the 'ice' has gone and our 'ship' is free!

II. Why and when does God show His power?

I have already said that it is the mind and hand of Satan that so often produce the difficulties that bind us in. Why does God allow this, seeing that He could, if He wished, destroy Satan and his work in a moment? It is because He wants us, His people, to learn the way of victory over Satan. The difficulties are therefore allowed for our instruction. And thank God, victory over Satan is not gained by our struggling against him. There is One Who has already done that, and gained a full and final victory over him. In His Cross the Lord Jesus Christ utterly overcame him, and is now seated in heaven, in the place of all authority and power, able and willing to share His victory with any—even the least and the weakest—who trust in Him. So for us, deliverance from Satan and all his work comes by claiming Christ's victory, not by struggling for our own. "*Christ (is) the power of God*" (I. Cor. 1.24). And in answer to our claim, God works.

III. For whom does God show His power?

His Word tells us that "*the eyes of the Lord run to and fro throughout the whole earth, to show himself strong in the behalf of them whose heart is perfect toward him*" (II. Chron. 16. 9). A "perfect" heart. That is not a heart that never sins, but one that is complete or undivided—wholly set upon God in reverence and love, in confidence and humble dependence; and a heart that wants only God's will—that does not even want the 'ice' to be broken up and the 'ship' to be released unless that can be for God's glory; a heart that does not vainly struggle to do everything for itself but brings all its needs to God in earnest prayer. No one can have such an attitude towards God if he has not first of all found peace with God through faith in the Lord Jesus Christ, and then asked that his heart might be cleansed from all selfish and sinful desires and that he might be filled with the Holy Spirit. Have you done this?

IV. If God's power, not our own, does the work, is there nothing at all for us to do?

Yes, there is one thing we must do—we must work *the work of faith.* We read that *God. . .worketh for him that waiteth for him*" (Isaiah 63. 4. R.V.). "Waiting" for God. That does not mean just being lazy, waiting until something happens. It means a continual attitude of faith and prayer, standing before God continually and asking that the victory of Jesus Christ may be granted us in our time of need. Our deliverance may not come at the moment when we first pray. We must continue waiting in faith. And, "*in due season we shall reap, if we faint not*" (Gal. 6. 9).

Do you see the way of releasing your 'ship' from the 'ice'? The boy or girl who knows how to claim the mighty victory of Calvary over all the power of Satan will certainly find release that others will never know, and will arrive at the 'South Pole' while others are still a long way behind, vainly trying by their own feeble explosions to break the 'ice' that holds up their progress.

For the Lion of Judah shall break every chain,
And give us the victory again and again.

Chapter Fourteen

PACK-ICE

WHO IS IN YOUR CROW'S-NEST?

"Trust in the Lord with all thine heart, and lean not upon thine own understanding. In all thy ways acknowledge him, and he shall direct thy paths" (Prov. 3. 5, 6).

NO ship can ever reach the Antarctic Continent without first passing through a great belt of what is known as pack-ice. This is ice which forms over the sea around the coasts during the winter, and then for one reason or another is broken up and carried by the wind and currents out to sea, like floating rafts—or 'floes' as they are called. Quite a long time before approaching land a ship encounters this enormous field of moving ice, and must somehow find a way through it.

The floes are sometimes quite small in area, and sometimes very large. The ice may be thin and easily broken—or many feet in thickness so that no ship can break it. Under the influence of the wind and the sea the floes at times pack closely together; at other times they spread out, with open water between them. If the gap of water—or 'lead' as it is called—is wide enough, the ship can sail along it. The ship may even be able to push the floes apart if they are not too large, and make a lead for herself. But there are times when the floes are so tightly packed or so large, and the ice so thick, that the ship can make no progress at all. She must then either wait until a lead opens, or, if it is possible, go back, and look for another lead in some other direction. The whole process is one of stops and starts.

Capt. Scott met with quite unusual trouble in the pack-ice. Very seldom did he find that he could sail for more than a few miles without being held up. He found that the best way to proceed was for one of the ship's officers to be stationed high up the mast, in the crow's-nest. From there the officer could see for quite a long distance, and could pick out the best route to follow in order to take advantage of the open leads of water. He would shout down his orders to the man at the helm, who would steer accordingly. He was, as it were, the eyes of the ship. He could see what those on deck could not see. But even he was very limited. He could only see a certain distance, and could never be really sure that the course he was following would end in open water. On one occasion, Capt. Scott wrote: *'We felt there was just a chance of getting through, but we have stuck half-way: advance and retreat are equally impossible.'*

On another occasion: *'I thought we had come to an end of our troubles. . . I did not for a moment suspect we should get into thick pack again behind the great sheets of open water we have crossed. . . but we have come up against an immense floe about as big as any we have seen, and we cannot move.'*

The whole process was full of surprises and disappointments. Sometimes they would be sailing towards a promising looking stretch of open water, but before they reached it the ice would mysteriously close and there would be no way through. Sometimes the reverse happened, and there would suddenly be an open way where before there was no way at all.

They were often so hemmed in by ice that they could not move, and with no open water anywhere in sight. The ship was halted on one occasion for five days, a helpless prisoner. What patience was needed at such times!

Capt. Scott wrote: '*What an exasperating game this is! One cannot tell what is going to happen in the next half or even quarter of an hour. At one moment everything looks flourishing; the next, one begins to doubt if it is possible to get through. . . We can see big lanes of open water further on, but we are hemmed in by the pack and cannot get to them.*'

You can easily see how necessary it was to trust the officer in the crow's-nest. Probably at times the rest of the party were inclined to blame him if the ship ran into a wall of ice and could not go further. But they all had confidence when Mr. Bowers was the officer on duty. They knew they could trust him to do the very best thing. If the ship came to a halt when he was on duty—well, there must be a good reason for it. But even he had his limits. He could not see and know everything, and so it often happened that what he hoped would be an open way proved a disappointment.

Now if you will open your Bible and read Numbers 9. 15-23, you will find that what we have been saying is something like the way in which God's people Israel journeyed—not through pack-ice, but through the wilderness. They did not decide their own movements. They had Someone Who gave them orders where to go, when to stop and when to move. They were guided by "the cloud." The cloud was the sign of God's presence among them.

Now the great advantage which they had as compared with Capt. Scott was this—the One Who was, so to speak, in the crow's-nest of their ship was God Himself, Who could see the whole way, right to the end of the journey, and knew exactly the best course to take. Even Mr. Bowers could see only a comparatively short distance over the ice, and with all his skill he was often baffled and did not know which way to go. Yet, in spite of their having so wonderful a guide, we find the children of Israel constantly grumbling and rebelling. No doubt they said things like this—'Why must we stop just here?' or, 'We are tired of this place; why can't we move on now?' or, 'Why can't we stay here longer?' or, 'Why are we being led along *this* path? It is obviously the wrong one.'

I am sure they said this kind of thing, because these are the things that *we* often say when God seeks to lead us on. We are full of questions and doubts as to the wisdom and rightness of His way, and all too often we allow our own foolish and impatient hearts to persuade us into taking some course different from that in which God is seeking to lead us. But everything depends upon the knowledge and ability of the one in charge; and we can be quite sure that the very wisest possible thing for us to do is to trust the directing of our lives absolutely into the care of our perfect, all-knowing, all-able God, and to follow where He leads, even if it looks to us to be wrong, and to stop as long as He stops, even though we think it would be better to go on.

Perfect trust in God and patience to wait for Him are the great needs of every one of us. The end of our own way is always sorrow and disappointment. *God's way is always right.*

But you may ask, if God sees the end from the beginning, why does He not lead us straight forward? Why do we find ourselves halted again and again so that we cannot move?

Capt. Scott says this very interesting thing about the pack-ice:

'One is much struck by our inability to find a cause for the periodic opening and closing of the floes. . . . In general, it seems to show that *our conditions are governed by remote causes.* Somewhere well north or south of us the wind may be blowing in some other direction. . . . One can only vaguely feel that things *are happening far beyond our horizon which directly affect our situation.'*

Why the sudden hold-up in our lives? Why the sudden opening of the way?

We cannot explain, as a rule; but it may be because of things happening elsewhere, out of our sight and knowledge. God is doing an immense work. He is controlling a multitude of lives—and He causes all things to work *together* for good to them that love Him (Rom. 8. 28). Perhaps we have to wait sometimes until other lives are ready to fit in with us—and we seem to be brought to a standstill, hemmed in on every side. And then all at once there comes release, a way opens and we can go forward. We do not know why; we are not aware of anything that has happened to cause the change, but there it is.

God has done it, because the time has come for us to take another step. But while we are waiting, are we blaming God for the delay as if He had made a mistake? And, when the way opens again, do we grumble because of the direction in which it leads?

If we do, we have not learned to trust in the Lord with all our heart, but we are leaning upon our own understanding. If we did but know it, that may be very often the chief reason why God allows us to be held up and to be led along strange and undesired ways. He wants above everything else to win our hearts' love and confidence—to save us from the folly of trusting in ourselves, and for our own good to teach us to trust wholly in Him only.

And, remember, He will not show us all the way ahead—just one step at a time. Why? Because if He showed us more, we might begin to feel we did not need Him so much. So He shuts us up to a life of faith, in which we have to trust Him moment by moment and to rely on Him for everything if we are to come safely through life's 'pack-ice' and reach the open water at the other side.

Do you think this is a hard and anxious way of living? No, it is the way of perfect rest. The Lord Jesus, more than any other who ever lived, was a Man of rest, and the secret was that He lived under the complete control of His Father, and depended utterly upon Him for everything, and therefore had no anxieties whatever: and He has given us His Holy Spirit to lead us in the same way.

Others in the Bible learned the lesson well, though none so perfectly as He. Abraham started out on a journey in obedience to God's call "*not knowing whither he went*" (Heb. 11. 8). He did not know the way, nor the destination; but he went a step at a time with God, and arrived safely. If you will read II. Sam. 5. 17-25, you will see David receiving instructions from One above, and being guided successfully through the 'pack-ice.' In verses 17-21, he was shown an open lead that took him straight through, but in verses 22-25 he had to go round another way.

In Acts 16. 6-10 you can read how Paul also was guided through. You can see him trying one way after another before he found one that brought him right through; but he found the way in the end, because he was seeking only God's way, not his own, and was utterly obedient to the Holy Spirit. Like his Master, he could say, "*I seek not mine own will, but the will of him that sent me*" (John 5. 30).

Such men will always get through their 'pack-ice' successfully, for they have learned how treacherous and how foolish are their own thoughts—and that "it is better to trust in the Lord than to put confidence in man" (Psa. 118. 8). Their message to us would be:

"Commit thy way unto the Lord; trust also in him, and he will bring it to pass" (Psa. 37. 5).

Now I wonder who is in the crow's-nest of your ship, directing your course? Are you there yourself?

Then you can be quite sure you are in for trouble! Why not ask the Lord Himself to be there, and to guide you in the way that you should go? He sees the way clearly, right to the end. He is the One Who is "*perfect knowledge*" (Job 36. 4). If you are prepared to accept His direction, even when He leads you by ways you do not understand or halts you when you would go forward; if you are prepared to trust and obey Him in everything: if you are willing to crown Him Lord of your life and to hand over entirely to Him the government of all your matters: if you are prepared to say, "*Not my will, but thine, be done*" (Luke 22. 42), and, "*Lord, what wilt thou have me to do?*" (Acts 9. 6, A.V.)—then you may be quite certain that He will gladly and readily respond to you, and will guide you unfailingly through your 'pack-ice,' and lead you right on, all the way to the 'South Pole.' Are you prepared to do that? If so, will you kneel down now and tell the Lord so?

The boy or girl who submits to the Lord Jesus Christ in every detail of his or her life will certainly arrive at the 'Pole' while others who do not do so are still hopelessly trying to find a way through their 'pack-ice.'

Do you want a Pilot? Signal then to Jesus.
Do you want a Pilot? Bid Him come on board.
For He will safely guide across the ocean wide,
Until you reach at last the Heavenly Harbour.

Chapter Fifteen

ICEBERGS

ARE YOU MELTING?

"Every one that exalteth himself shall be humbled; and he that humbleth himself shall be exalted" (Luke 14. 11).

Jesus said: "Learn of me; for I am meek and lowly in heart" (Matt. 11. 29).

MOST things in the world have some use or other, but I cannot discover that icebergs have any use whatever. They are only a nuisance and a danger. The seas of the Antarctic are full of them. They are like floating islands of ice. Capt. Scott sailed past one which was over twenty miles long! An iceberg floats with only about one-eighth of its total mass above the water, so that a berg that appears to be 200 feet high above water will reach very much further below the surface. Imagine the weight and power of that, as it is carried along by wind and current! It travels along, crashing through pack-ice and anything else that gets in its way, and woe betide the ship that is unfortunate enough to be in the line of its advance! Many times, Capt. Scott had anxious moments, wondering if his ship would escape an advancing iceberg, but happily the danger was avoided every time.

What is an iceberg? Well, it is really only a mass of frozen water—much like the water of the sea in which it floats, though in a different form. Now (whatever we may think of the sea in a storm!) we can at any rate say that, as compared with an iceberg, the water of the sea is useful. Among other uses, it carries the ships that sail upon it—whereas icebergs would sink them. But more than that; water is, so to speak, united and friendly. No part of it seems to be fighting for itself against the rest. It all flows together so smoothly so that you cannot see the different drops or pick out a distinct and separate piece. If you draw out some and then pour it back, it at once flows into the rest and loses itself. The drops unite together in a way that seems to say they are all glad to lose their separateness and to become one with all the others. When we find this same attitude among Christians, we call it 'fellowship.'

But you can never think of an iceberg as being in any sense friendly. It is a distinct and separate thing; it has its own boundaries, it goes its own way, it seems to say to all around it, 'Get out of my way; I keep myself to myself; I have nothing to do with anything else.' If it does come into contact with anything else, there is a clash. It seems to glory in being alone, and on it goes, solitary and unfriendly, pushing everything else out of its way. A large one often breaks up into smaller ones, but every part thus formed becomes another source of trouble, crashing its way along, sometimes colliding with other icebergs as if fighting them, but never on any account uniting with them. Every one is a separate thing, and the longer they go on their course the more trouble will they make –*until something changes their nature.*

How can an iceberg change its nature? Only by melting. And as it does so, little by little the water flows from it into the sea and loses itself among all the other drops of water there; and the iceberg becomes smaller and smaller, until in due course it all turns to water, and then—and only then—has it become really safe and useful.

It is very humiliating, isn't it? To feel that you are only safe and useful when you have died right out and have become nothing. Nevertheless, that is one of the greatest spiritual lessons we all have to learn. When it is really "not I, but Christ," we are quite safe and God can use us to great blessing.

I do not want to be a spiritual 'iceberg,' do you?

Yet, I fear many people are such, though they may not realize it. They are people who have not learned to 'flow.' They like to keep themselves to themselves, to hold to their own thoughts, to choose their own way and follow their own inclinations. They may even pride themselves on being independent, on being able to get along very well without anybody's help, on knowing exactly what they think and having no need of the advice of others, even though older and more experienced than themselves.

No one can teach them anything, and unless others agree with them and are willing to go their way there is no possibility of working together with them. They often seem as if they cannot trust anyone else, and will not confide in others or share their matters with them. They are hard and set, independent and separate. They seem unable to unite with others, and though others of their company are flowing together in happy fellowship, they themselves remain apart and distinct. They cannot, or will not, let go of their own things. In pursuing their own way, they often cause great harm to others.

There is only one remedy for such 'iceberg' people, and until they find it, they will be a problem to everybody. They must learn to 'flow,' and to do this they must 'melt.'

There never was another man who 'flowed' so wonderfully as the Lord Jesus when He was here on earth. People of all kinds and classes could be at ease with Him, provided their hearts were open and sincere and ready to recognize that He could help them. Though He was so very different from them all in the holiness of His nature, so that He might have been perfectly justified in claiming to be distinct and separate from others, yet there was nothing about Him that clashed with the simple-hearted people who came to Him. He could share with them in their sorrows and their problems; He could come down to their level and be in perfect sympathy with them. He loved them; and in Him was no proud attitude that seemed to say 'I am better than you.' Indeed, He was the One Who could say of Himself, "*I am meek and lowly in heart*" (Matt. 11. 29). His heart flowed out to them, and they gladly trusted Him and opened their hearts to Him.

But there were some with whom it was different; Pharisees, scribes, chief priests, lawyers. Many of these were stubborn and proud in heart. They kept themselves to themselves. They resented anything that seemed to threaten their own interests. They thought they knew better than anyone else. Their pride was wounded by the example and the words of Jesus. They resisted His teaching, and in the end, they caused Him to be put to death rather than humble themselves and confess that He was right and they were wrong. 'Self' was their great concern. They would not let go of their own position or opinions. They were 'icebergs' that would not 'melt.' If you read Luke 18. 9-14, you will find there two men, one of whom was an 'iceberg' and one whose heart 'flowed.' I think you will easily decide which is which.

There were some, too, who were not positively wicked men fighting against God, but who were nevertheless spiritual 'icebergs.' Saul of Tarsus was one. He says, *"I verily thought. . . that I ought to do many things. . ."* (Acts 26.9). No one could convince him he was wrong. He needed no one's help or advice. And so he went on his way, persecuting the followers of the Lord Jesus and bringing damage and hurt wherever he came. And then suddenly he met the Lord Himself, as you can read in Acts 9.—and in the fierce heat of that blazing light that shone into his heart the 'iceberg' began to melt very quickly, and, greatly humbled, he said, "Lord, what wilt thou have me to do?" From that moment his heart began to 'flow'—first in love to his Lord and then in love to men; and in humble and willing service he poured out his life for others.

What is it that makes anyone an 'iceberg'?

I think the chief cause is pride.

We think of ourselves more highly than we ought to think, and have no real sense of need. We feel we are sufficient in ourselves, and while others around us are flowing together and being helped by one another, we go on our way proudly confident and alone. We must be humble if we are to 'flow'—and until we are, we shall be a danger to the things of God. In this matter we have to learn to know our own hearts, for there is far more pride in every one of us than we realise.

There is only one way whereby our hard, 'iceberg' hearts can be 'melted,' and that is by allowing the grace of the Lord Jesus to work in us, producing in us His own meek and lowly character. As He does that, we shall become more and more like Him—more truly humble, less concerned about our own things and more desirous of 'flowing' with others, for the good of all. It is wonderful to watch spiritual 'icebergs' gradually 'melting'! Self becomes less and less, Christ becomes more and more in them; the sense that they need others grows, and love towards others expresses itself more and more. Less and less do 'I,' 'me' and 'my' govern the life, and where before it was difficult for simple folk to get on with them, gradually this difficulty disappears and hearts flow together in loving fellowship.

We cannot change ourselves.

Capt. Scott noticed many icebergs of an unusual shape, and at first wondered what accounted for the difference. He decided that they were simply bergs that had capsized and were floating bottom upwards. But they were icebergs still—just as unfriendly and dangerous. So are our proud hearts, however they may twist and turn. The only remedy for them is the Spirit of the Lord working in them to change them, and He will most surely and gladly do that work if we will give Him the opportunity.

I must tell you, before I close, of one more very common sight along the Antarctic coasts. Many an iceberg lies stranded in shallow water, having continued on its proud way until it found itself stuck fast and unable to move—like some crippled giant, helpless and ashamed. Formerly so dangerous and feared—now a captive, an object of pity rather than of fear. Many a proud heart has brought its owner to a place of shame and disappointment, and there is no way of escape except one—the one by which alone a stranded iceberg can escape. It can melt, and flow away unseen and be lost in the great ocean.

So there is deliverance for the proud heart, if it will humble itself and yield itself to the Lord Jesus. By letting go to Him, and, so to speak, dying, it will find, as if by a resurrection, a life of usefulness and love that it never knew before.

There are many stranded spiritual 'icebergs' in the world –people who know they have failed and missed the way and that they can do nothing to deliver themselves out of the place and condition to which they have come, and yet will not humble their hearts enough to confess their wrong and seek God's forgiveness and deliverance. If only they would believe it, humility is their way of escape. *"Humble yourselves therefore under the mighty hand of God, that he may exalt you in due season"* (I. Pet. 5. 6).

Now even though you may not at the moment feel very strongly that you are an 'iceberg', will you kneel and ask the Lord that everything that He sees in you that is proud, or hard, or selfish, or unloving, may by His Spirit be made to 'melt'; and that He will so fill you with His own love and meekness that you may be one whose heart 'flows' out in love and fellowship and helpfulness towards others around you?

The boy or girl who has most of the meekness and lowliness of the Lord Jesus will certainly reach the 'South Pole' before others.

Oh, to be saved from myself, dear Lord,
Oh, to be lost in Thee.
Oh, that it may be no more I,
But Christ that lives in me.

Chapter Sixteen

KILLER WHALES

IS IT WORTH WHILE PRAYING?

"Ye have not, because ye ask not"
(James 4. 2).

"Ask, and ye shall receive, that your joy may be full" (John 16. 24).

BEFORE going any further, will you please read the thrilling story in Acts 12. 1-19? I want you to notice especially verses 12 and 5:

v. 12. "*Many were gathered together and were praying.*"
v. 5. "*Prayer was made earnestly* (or, without ceasing)."

There are many mysteries in connection with prayer, and the above verses suggest two of them:

1. Why did the Christians in Acts 12—and why do we—need *to gather together* to pray? Is it not sufficient if we each pray alone?
2. Why did they—and why do we—need to *keep on* praying about a matter? Why does not God answer at once?

Now if I tell you an Antarctic story, I think you will be able to feel the answers to these questions even if you cannot really explain them in words.

When Capt. Scott and his party sailed South from New Zealand, they at last reached a point where the sea was largely covered with thick ice, and the ship could go no further. There she lay alongside a large sheet of ice, just like a ship alongside the quay in a harbour. Some of the men disembarked and walked on the ice, one of them having his camera with him to photograph anything of special interest. Suddenly he saw in the water close to the ship a number of creatures known as killer whales—great sea monsters about 30 feet long, with enormous heads and mouths, and possessing what is said to be the most terrible and fearsome set of teeth in the world. These whales live in large numbers in the Antarctic seas, and go about in packs a hundred strong and more. They feed upon other creatures such as seals and penguins. One bite from those awful teeth and that would be the end of any poor victim.

The photographer saw the whales swimming in the sea and noticed that from time to time they lifted their heads out of the water as if to take a good look round about. He became tremendously interested and was very busy preparing his camera to take a photograph of them, when, all at once, as if acting upon a word of command, all the whales disappeared. There was a moment's pause, and then came a series of terrific bumps under the ice on which the explorer was standing. Bump, bump, bump! Bang, bang, bang!

The men on the ship could hear the booming noise as the whales rose and struck the ice with their backs. All at once the sheet of ice began to break into pieces, and up from the water that separated the pieces appeared here and there the cruel head of a whale, with mouth open ready to devour anything within reach.

The photographer waited no longer, but fled for his life, and managed to get back to the ship; and the whales, being disappointed of the meal they had hoped for, departed.

The writer of our book says: *'The facts that the whales could display such deliberate cunning, that they were able to break ice of such thickness (at least 2 ½ feet), and that they could act in unison, were a revelation to us. It is clear that they are endowed with singular intelligence. . . .'*

Yes, indeed—the whales seem to be wiser in their world than we do in ours. I am quite sure that the same result would not have been obtained if first one and then another whale had come along and struck the ice once or twice and then turned away because nothing happened. They knew the secrets of successful attack, and can teach us a great deal, especially about prayer. There are some very important differences between the whales' knocking on the ice and our praying to our Father Who is in heaven, but we will not deal with those now. What we want is to see how the story helps us to answer the questions which we asked at the beginning.

Firstly: why come together to pray? The whales show us the value of acting 'corporately' –that is, all together, as a team, as one body. There is a wonderful strength gained from acting together. We know this is true in ordinary matters of life and it is very specially true in spiritual things. We greatly need one another, and any Christian who thinks he can get along very well on his own is making a great mistake.

We read in Deut. 32. 30, that *"one shall chase a thousand, but two shall put ten thousand to flight."* Is there not something wrong with the arithmetic of that? Should not twice as many chasers mean twice the number put to flight? But this verse says that two together shall chase ten times as many enemies as one acting alone. It is exactly like that, not only in prayer but in all spiritual things.

If you don't believe it, try it! Have you been praying about something and seemed to get no answer?

Well, have you a brother or sister or friend who loves the Lord? If so, ask them to pray with you about that matter, and it will be a surprise if something does not happen.

Something happened for Peter in Acts 12 when the believers gathered together to pray! *"If two of you shall agree. . . as touching anything that they shall ask, it shall be done for them of my Father which is in heaven"* (Matt. 18. 19).

Then secondly: why keep on praying?

The whales show us the value of 'importunity,' that is, of continuing steadfastly in prayer. We so easily grow tired of praying because the answer seems long in coming. Well—the whales kept on until the ice broke; and the Lord Jesus told us that *"men ought always to pray and not to faint"* (Luke 18. 1)

You see, we must not think that prayer is merely a means of persuading God to do things for us. He would swiftly answer if that were all. But He wants us to grow in faith and has valuable lessons for us to learn, one of which is that in the spiritual world, which we touch when we really pray, there are strong resisting forces that must be overcome, and that do not readily yield.

Every fresh blow of the whales did something to weaken the ice until at last its resistance was broken; and in our case every fresh blow in prayer brings nearer the moment when our 'ice' will break and God can give us the desire of our hearts.

Have you given up praying for something or for someone, because you have decided that prayer is useless? Will you not begin again and ask God to give you grace to pray daily until the final blow 'breaks the ice'?

But perhaps you feel that the prayers of a boy or girl are not very important, because you are only young and cannot pray very well. Don't you think it likely that there may have been some young whales on the scene in our story?

If there were, I am sure they joined in—and every blow they gave would have helped towards the breaking of the ice, if only by a little. In the matter of prayer, though, there is a very big difference to be noted. One of the most wonderful things about prayer is this, that when even the feeblest person truly prays to God, *it is the power of God Himself* that comes into action—not the power of the one who prays.

The Lord Jesus said: "If ye abide in me, and my words abide in you, ask whatsoever ye will, and *it shall be done unto you"* (John 15. 7). So even if you are only young and weak, you can be one of those who ask and it shall be done, even unto you. We have already quoted Matt. 18. 19: "If two of you shall agree. . .as touching anything that they shall ask, *it shall be done for them of my Father*, which is in heaven." "Done for them of (that is, by) my Father"!

What can He not do? There is nothing too hard for Him!

The prayer of the smallest and least among us, if it is really a prayer from the heart to our heavenly Father, can bring the power of God into action. Isn't prayer wonderful? Why don't we practice it much more than we do?

The boy or girl who prays most will certainly be the first to reach the 'South Pole'. But we must not think of travelling there *alone.* When Capt. Scott went to the Pole, he had four companions with him; he certainly could not have arrived there without their help. We must travel *together,* in company with others who are pressing on in the same way; and perhaps more than anything else, praying together will help us to the goal.

I believe God answers prayer;
I am sure God answers prayer;
I have proved God answers prayer;
Glory to His Name

www.ingramcontent.com/pod-product-compliance
Lightning Source LLC
Chambersburg PA
CBHW071636050426
42443CB00028B/3345

9780988328051